TALENT
and the Secret Life of Teams

TERRY PETTIT

Printed by Walsworth Publishing Co.

Cover photograph by Gary Meyer, used with the permission of the University of Nebraska Athletic Department.

The following first appeared in *Coaching Volleyball,* a publication of the American Volleyball Coaches Association:

    "Finding a Path Into Coaching"

    "The Development of the Extraordinary Coach"

    "The Difference Between Talent and Skill"

    "Why I Love Great Setters"

    " Snakes, Recruits, and Serendipity"

    ''The Final Phase In A Coaching Life"

    "Make Room for the Beach"

The following first appeared in *The Lincoln Journal-Star:*

    "In Breathing and Conspiring Together, The Glory"

    "Coaching and Parenting"

ISBN: 978-1-4276-3535-8

A special thanks to Nancy Evans Hammel and Paul Hammel for editing and advice and to Sandra Denneler for the layout and graphic design.

I would also like to thank the athletic departments at the University of Nebraska, Creighton University, the University of Denver, and Colorado State University for the opportunity to mentor coaches and student leaders at those institutions, and to the Talent Plus Organization, for their support in leadership development.

Lastly, I would like to thank the women that I had the opportunity to coach at the University of Nebraska, who were remarkable in their effort, and who continue to make a difference wherever they are today.

For Anne, Katherine, and Emma

There are two ways of being creative. One can sing and dance. Or one can create an environment in which singers and dancers flourish. – Warren Bennis

CONTENTS

FOREWORD

Beyond the wins and championships, what Terry Pettit brought to the Nebraska Volleyball program was a vision. Long before anyone else saw what collegiate women's volleyball could be, Terry put into motion what is Nebraska Volleyball today. There isn't a program in the country – high school or college – that hasn't been positively influenced by his efforts.

His program was built with great athletes and paying attention to the details. I always believed Terry could take his players and beat your team and then turn around and take your players and beat his own team. That's not just an understanding of the x's and o's, it's understanding the big picture. Just as his teams forced opposing coaches and teams out of their comfort zones, Terry's words will do the same. Read this book and you will want to re-examine the most important aspect of coaching: the ability to lead.

Mary Wise, Head Volleyball Coach
University of Florida

INTRODUCTION

In 1997 my assistant coaches, Cathy Noth and Nikki Best, and I were seated in the dressing room at Texas A&M University after meeting with the Nebraska women's volleyball team, which had left to begin stretching before warming up for a match with the Aggies.

We had just lost two matches in a row; something that had not happened in several years and that had created some anxiety among the coaching staff. A week earlier we had lost our two primary passers to injury and had to pull a promising but inexperienced freshman out of a redshirt season. A&M had a talented team, and as I looked at the paint peeling from the walls of the old locker room, the prospects for turning things around in the upcoming match were problematic at best.

We still had a great deal of talent on the court, but it was a team built of exceptional parts: an outstanding outside hitter and physical presence in Nancy Meendering, an All-American setter in Fiona Nepo, a dynamic middle blocker in Megan Korver, and two consistent passers in Jamie Krondak and Renee Saunders who were now unavailable with injuries. It was like having a plane with two powerful jet engines, an experienced pilot, and no wheels to taxi.

I remember asking Cathy and Nikki how much money someone would have to pay them to live in the dilapidated locker room for a year. We all agreed the figure would be north of a million dollars. The question was a way of acknowledging that there is only so much you can take charge of as a coach. It was way of saying that if we were going to win the match, there would have to be some serendipity in the play of our most experienced players. We would have to compete, win, and leave town before A&M realized how vulnerable we were at serve reception without our two primary passers.

They do not teach you how to respond to situations like this in coaching or leadership manuals. One of my favorite quotes is by leadership guru Warren Bennis who said that *leadership can't be taught, but it can be learned.* I feel the same about coaching, and I'll bet if you ask the best chefs in New Orleans or the best racecar drivers at Indy they would say something similar about their passions. So why write a book on coaching and leadership? I think there are at least a couple of answers to that question.

These essays, columns, poems, and letters reflect my own journey into coaching. Each entry is part of a story of how I came to see the challenges in my coaching development. In some ways, the writing approaches fiction because when I recall the experiences in my memory they are framed by my current understanding of what happened. When I read my own writing it strikes me as more calm and patient than the person who came to those insights.

My goal is not to persuade you to my point of view or coaching philosophy, but rather to stimulate you to reflect on your own story and begin to take responsibility for your own coaching development if you have not already done so. I am the product of a romantic view of education, which centers on the idea that if we focus on any specific discipline, such as literature, we are likely to gain a better understanding of other disciplines such as music or history. My coaching owes as much to reading Thomas Hardy as it does to listening to John Wooden, as much to reading Borges as it does to watching Charlie Rose interview Duke basketball coach Mike Krzyzewski. I cannot look at a painting by Georgia O'Keefe without thinking about color, spaces in the imagination, and intuitive intelligence.

That is why the structure of this book moves from essays to poems to journal entries and fiction, and the tone moves from serious to didactic to self-deprecating. The variety of structure and point of view are who I am, and how I have thought about coaching and leadership for the past thirty years.

As for the match against Texas A&M, setter Fiona Nepo began the match with three consecutive jump serves resulting in service aces, putting the Aggies on their heels and setting the tone for a remarkable turnaround in a memorable season. Her leadership in that situation also is a metaphor for two themes that continually emerge throughout these pages: talent and grace.

Terry Pettit
November 15, 2008

FINDING A PATH INTO COACHING

There is something heroic in wanting to be a coach. It requires as much ego as it takes to write a poem and there are far more risks. Who would take on a job description that encompasses teaching, motivating, recruiting, scouting, fund-raising, negotiating, staff development, managing team travel, compliance, developing a vision and philosophy, marketing, practice planning, and communicating with parents who believe their child has replaced Pluto as the ninth planet? Yet many of us come eagerly to this profession, sometimes because of the impact a coach has had on us, even one we did not particularly enjoy at the time. I am reminded of this qualification by some of my former players.

My first coach was my father who managed my Little League team when I was 9 through 12 years old and growing up in a small town in northwest Indiana. There aren't a lot of things he did that today's parents sometimes associate with coaching. He didn't give motivational speeches. He didn't force me to practice each day or shuttle me to developmental camps during the summer. He didn't put me at pitcher or shortstop when I had the arm strength for a utility infielder. He didn't even seem to be disappointed when I chose not to play organized baseball after Little League when I began caddying and playing golf instead. My decision did not affect his enjoyment of coaching baseball, and he continued to coach at one level or another into his 70s.

My second coach was Coach Rawlings, the South Ward Junior High basketball coach who reflected the culture of what youth sport was in the 1950s. He had a flattop haircut. He was an ex-Marine.

1

He called me "little guy" and he did not allow the players on his team to drink water during practice because he was afraid we would get "waterlogged." (Concerns about dehydration replaced concerns about being waterlogged about the time Gatorade was invented.) He witnessed one event that no coach should ever have to experience. In 1959 one of his seventh-grade players who was my teammate collapsed after practice and died of a heart attack. The boy, James Corrigan, had been diagnosed with a heart murmur but had forged his parent's signature on the physical form so that he could be part of a team.

I had a rather uninspiring athletic career as a high school golfer who was good enough to play on the high school varsity for two years and then at a small liberal arts college in Indiana as a freshman. My interest in e.e. cummings, the Berrigan brothers, late-night discussions about philosophy and sex, witnesses and marches against the war in Vietnam, and the enthusiastic embracement of a place where you could raise a crow in your dorm room, study and debate anything with like-minded students over beer, and take road trips for sweet rolls gradually replaced athletic competition as a focus.

Graduate school followed where I spent a year at a Brethren seminary outside Chicago memorizing eight of the twelve apostles, learning the Hebrew phrase, *tohu vavohu* (order out of chaos), which would come in handy later in coaching, working at the Illinois State Psychiatric Clinic as a psychiatric aide, and protesting on the fringes of the 1968 Democratic convention. At some point, probably after the first semester grades came out and I was in danger of losing a fellowship, I came to believe that I wanted to be a writer and that I needed to move on.

Following two years of alternative service as a conscientious objector, I enrolled in the Creative Writing Workshop at the University of Arkansas where I wrote poetry, explored the creeks of the nearby Boston Mountains, taught English at a junior high to pay for my tuition, and graduated with a Master of Fine Arts in poetry. Coaching was further from my mind than string theory.

So my first coaching job was by chance. In the spring of 1974 I toured the Southeast, from Mississippi to Maryland, in a yellow Volkswagen exploring the back roads that are home to small liberal arts colleges in the hopes of finding a teaching job during a recession. Two weeks of travel produced three possibilities: one at community college on Maryland's eastern shore where I had mistaken hush puppies for shrimp at a lunch with the academic dean, another at an all-girls school in Radford, Virginia, and the third (which I eventually took) at a Methodist junior college in Louisburg, North Carolina, where I was hired to teach four courses, coach men's golf, men's tennis, women's volleyball, and be the faculty advisor of the student literary magazine.

Louisburg College, the oldest two-year college in the United States, is located in the Piedmont of North Carolina about forty-five miles north of Raleigh, and was stuck in a time warp during the early 1970s that reminded me of a culture not unlike the one depicted in *Gone With the Wind.* While the public schools had recently been integrated, that did not extend to the plumbing in residential neighborhoods. Statues in town honored Civil War heroes in rebel hats, and the local golf course, where I coached the college team, did not allow blacks on the course unless they had a fairway mower in tow.

Coaching men's tennis and golf was interesting in that it gave me insight into the male psyche where there is frequently an excuse when something goes wrong. When a senior lost 0-6, 0-6, 0-6 in a challenge match for the right to play in the No. 6 singles spot because his "racquet was strung too tight," I began to have an appreciation for the fresh inexperience and eagerness that was the countenance of many of the young women on the volleyball team.

This was 1974, a year and a half after the enactment of Title IX. The idea behind Title IX was so revolutionary that when the president of the college asked me to coach the volleyball team, I assumed he meant men. Women's sport was confined to GAA play days once a semester where girls donned pinnies and played two-dribble basketball trying not to be too aggressive less they be a labeled "tomboys," a concept that now seems as anachronistic as a dowry.

There were twenty-two women at the organizational meeting for women's volleyball, and none of them had ever played before. Only a handful had played any form of organized sport. Two of them thought they were joining the "soccerball" team and most of them came because of the free T-shirt advertised on the handwritten poster we placed in the

3

cafeteria and the dormitories. It *was* a nice T-shirt. I had a local high school teacher silk screen a design from *Volleyball Magazine* that had several images of a spiker making an approach.

There were some organizational challenges. The nets, which doubled as tennis nets, were heavy enough to catch a tuna and the standards were metal poles sunk into portland cement. It took two people to wheel them into place and they had to be tied off to the bleachers to keep them from wobbling onto the court. We had one volleyball, my own, a Tachikara SV-5W. The rubber balls the school had provided would be the fodder for lawsuits in a dodge ball game. The tower that we used for a referee stand was borrowed from the baseball coach and stood 6 feet above the net where the referee (who also played right field for the baseball team) looked down upon the court as if he were a lifeguard.

The biggest challenge was not the equipment, but the players themselves and the lack of opportunity they had been given prior to Title IX. Two players missed practice on the first Friday to go home to watch a football game. They weren't being subordinate; they had never been a part of something where there were expectations and required behaviors to be a part of the club. Another player had never been out of the county. Her first bus ride to an away match at North Carolina Central in Durham was the equivalent of a moon shot to her. When I noticed that she was not warming up with the rest of the team after we arrived, I found her sitting in the bus, embarrassed because she had "wet her pants" in all the excitement. She not only got off the bus, but went on to become a starter and later earned a master's degree. She is now a social worker in another county in North Carolina.

It would be easy to focus on all the things that wouldn't appear appropriate today. The team sat in lawn chairs along the sideline and slept in sleeping bags in the opponent's locker room on road trips. Because there was no travel budget, we ate pimento cheese sandwiches packed by the cafeteria for meals. We frequently had to set up the nets at an opponent's court when we wanted to warm up a half hour before the match. Milk and cookies with the opposing team followed competition. There was no trainer and no one got taped. When Jeannie Lynch suffered a shoulder separation, a teammate put it back in place and she continued playing. The state director of officials had to be persuaded that it was legal to back set the ball. The uniforms were handmade from a bolt of cloth we bought in Raleigh that didn't match the school colors. Most schools had a JV team as well as a varsity.

If the players were fledglings, the coaches were too. I remember lying awake one night trying to figure out all the tactical options in a 4-2 serve-reception pattern. As you may know, there aren't many. I found two. Your best attackers either precede the setter or follow the setter. This determines whether they side-out twice on the left or twice on the right. Because a team was allowed only three contacts including the block, it was rare to transition to an attack after a ball had been touched by the block. There was a very real tactical advantage to not blocking.

Volleyball coaches focused almost entirely on training individual fundamentals. Team systems were off in the future with video, Russian leapers, and Lycra. Someone who could attack the ball from the weak-side was as rare as a comet. There were not many self-help books on coaching volleyball. You learned on-the-fly or if you were lucky, you could bounce ideas off the men's basketball coach, which I did.

His name was Enid Drake and he was a former minor league catcher. The only thing slower than his walk was his speech. He wouldn't speak for several seconds after I asked him a question. At the time I thought he was old, but he was probably only 40 and would go on to coach for another twenty-five years. I would give up my fly rod and retirement plan to be as young as he was the day I first walked into his office.

After the first two weeks of practice in 1974, I went into Enid's office to ask him a question. We had been drilling on serve and serve-reception for eleven consecutive practices to the exclusion of everything else. In the first few days we had made significant progress, well, as much progress as you can make with one official ball and the others requiring the players to wrap ace bandages on their arms. But we had gone flat. Following the initial enthusiasm for playing volleyball or "soccerball" or whatever they thought they were playing, the players stopped improving. Their eyes glazed over and it looked like maybe the people who argued against having girls compete in organized sport were right. Maybe girls just couldn't take it. Maybe they weren't wired to do the tough stuff. Maybe they weren't mentally tough. Maybe I was an idiot.

5

I put all this to Enid in the form of a question as he sat behind his oak desk on the second floor of Woolen Gym. He listened and rocked, but he didn't say anything for a long time. So long, that I began to wonder if I forgot to ask the question. But after hitting the spittoon at his feet for the third time, he looked at me with that wide grin that sat on the limb of a tree in Alice's rabbit hole. And then the grin spoke. "Terry, you know they need fundamentals. I know they need fundamentals. But what these kids really need to know is that this game is fun." Then the grin went away as quickly as the flash from a firefly and I thanked him and was out the door.

We adjusted. We introduced spiking. We had more fun. But despite our newfound enthusiasm we lost the first game Louisburg College ever played in college volleyball, 15-0. We didn't even rotate. I'm not sure that we even had an attempted assist. We lost the match 2-0. We didn't have video or statistics to evaluate. We didn't over-analyze or switch to another system. We learned the same lesson volleyball teams have been learning at every level since the game was invented. You play to the level you pass. The loss allowed our players to gain a perspective on why we were spending so much time on serve-reception. Because they now understood on a much more personal level, their concentration improved and three weeks later we passed the ball well enough to beat the same team on their home court.

My conversation with Enid was my first experience at being mentored as a coach by anyone but my father. And, ironically, the message was not all that different from what my father taught me in Little League when he wasn't doing all those things parents want coaches to do now. He was teaching me that the game is fun, and it is more fun when you pay attention to details. Sometimes you have to teach people how to spike if you want them to stick around and learn to pass. Sometimes you look the other way when your kids are sneaking out the bedroom window during the dog days of August to go play pick-up in the park. Sometimes you have to tell someone that they can be great at something even before they've done anything on the court to indicate they could be good. Sometimes you need to give a person the room to develop her own dreams.

Almost every week I get an e-mail from someone who wants to be a coach or wants to build a program or wants to find the key to becoming exceptional. Having someone like Enid Drake to bounce ideas off of helps. Reading books about coaching can help. Working camps with great coaches can help. Working beneath or alongside an experienced head coach can help. Going to workshops with other great coaches can help. All these things can help, but the most important thing in the development of a coach or an athlete or a leader is that at some point she makes a decision to take charge of her own development. The coach or athlete becomes her own university and laboratory. She is constantly thinking, reading, prodding, and re-evaluating her own coaching. The key is that everything she is doing has an application to her development. She is not waiting for the perfect job. She is not waiting until the right position opens up. Her growth is not dependent upon budgets, number of scholarships, conferences, or the benevolence of athletic administrators. She is getting better, taking risks, failing, and learning from her mistakes.

And that is why the best coaches are unique. Their philosophy, methodology, even their vision of the game is an outgrowth of their own strengths and experiences. There is no universal best way to coach. There is no best system. The best coaches know who they are and don't spend a lot of time worrying about the talents they don't have. They learn from what they see but they don't mimic what they see. They are smart enough to change ideas and tactics as the game evolves but wise enough to avoid doing anything to be part of a trend.

This can happen at a small junior college in North Carolina. It can happen at a high school in Utah or a university in Nebraska. You can find insight into coaching in architecture and psychology and the sermon on Sunday. The person sitting next to you on a plane to Cincinnati might say something that gives you insight into one of your players or recommend a movie that changes your perspective on endgame. A basketball coach or a cartoon tiger named Hobbes can mentor you. It is all out there waiting for you to be heroic with.

MENTORED INTO COACHING

I grew up with a father who wanted to be a coach. He never told me this, but he didn't have to. My father worked as a milkman for a local dairy, running a home-delivery route five and six days a week. He was paid every other Monday, and after work on payday we would drive north through the county to Gary, Indiana, where he would cash his check at a Sears, Roebuck and Co., and my brothers and I would ride the escalators at Sears, and window-shop at all the shoe and novelty stores on Broadway where the featured item in almost every window, much to my amazement, was a 35mm camera no bigger than a bar of soap that our aunt would give us when she returned from a vacation to exotic locations outside Indiana.

Some days our trip ended with a visit to the Gary Bookstore where we would each choose a book to take home. I was an avid Hardy Boys fan and my brother Jack was equally enthusiastic about the Chip Hilton series. One Monday, after cashing my father's check and eating hamburgers at local café, as I was admiring the cover to the Hardy Boys' *The House on the Cliff,* my father handed me a copy of Garland F. Pinholster's *Encyclopedia of Basketball Drills.* I played basketball. We had a basketball court in the backyard, and we frequently went downtown to the Community building to watch the high school team play, but a book on basketball drills wasn't my idea of a good summer read.

He didn't tell me I had to choose the book; he was offering it as a suggestion. And so it was two more weeks before I had the chance to read about Frank and Joe Hardy and the secret of *The House on the Cliff.*

In the car on the way home I paged through the chapters and diagrams of plays and drills. It might as well have been written in Portuguese for all I could get out of it. I assumed my father handed me the book as a subtle reminder that I should be practicing more on the clay court that he built in the backyard. I should be doing more chin-ups on the wooden dowel he had placed in our closet. It wasn't until I had grown out of the Hardy Boys, fallen in love with poetry, and began teaching at a college in North Carolina that it occurred to me why he handed me a book on basketball drills when I was too young to appreciate it. It was what he wished he could have chosen to be if he hadn't gone to war just out of high school, if he hadn't spent four years in the Pacific, if he hadn't been a milkman, if he had been given the opportunity to go to college.

He wanted to be a coach, and in many ways, he was. He coached all three sons in Little League and Babe Ruth League baseball. He developed creative teaching aides to help us learn the fundamentals of baseball and basketball. He built a life-sized pitch-back out of stretched inner tubes woven onto a wooden frame long before a smaller aluminum version was available in sporting goods stores. More importantly, he taught me the importance of attention to detail and the advantage of preparation long before I discovered the same elements in Sun Tzu's *The Art of War.*

There are three brothers in my family. My brother Jack is three years younger than I and was a standout pitcher in baseball and point guard in basketball. Following an all-conference career at Crown Point High School, he received an athletic scholarship to play both sports at Valparaiso University.

My youngest brother, Paul, is four years younger than Jack and while he had the same introduction and encouragement in sport as his older brothers, he developed interests in automobiles and 4-H that continue to this day. From the time that Jack and I were 10 or so, we took turns helping my father on the milk route, particularly on Fridays and Saturdays which were his most difficult days because people and stores stocked up for the weekend. My father left for work at 2:30 a.m. after having breakfast with my mom who would wake one of us at 5:30 a.m.

We would get dressed then lie back down on the couch in the living room until we were awakened by the changing gears on the Divco milk truck as it approached our neighborhood. Lying on the couch in that half-sleep state was my first introduction to ambivalence. Sleep to a growing teenager is wonderful, and yet I also enjoyed the conversations and time with my father in the early morning, just the two of us with the Divco's headlights sweeping the streets of our small town in the hour just before dawn.

Sometimes there was instruction on how to place the half-gallon on a porch so it would be easy for the people asleep inside to retrieve it. Sometimes the milk was carried inside and placed in the refrigerator so an older person didn't have to risk bad weather and icy steps. Sometimes we talked about the bad penmanship that left us wondering whether the people asleep wanted two-dozen eggs or cottage cheese without legs. Once, when there was limited availability of milk because of a strike, I picked up a note that read: *"I know that milk is scarce so if the children at the school need milk please take mine and give it to them. If, however, they have plenty then please leave me an extra gallon and a half."* That was one of my first lessons in human nature.

The best thing about riding in the milk truck were the games we played, some of them word games and some of them games of perception. On one occasion my father asked me, "What was the name on the front of the refrigerator that you just placed that quart of milk in?" In the beginning I wasn't very good at answering his questions because I didn't focus on the details of what I was doing. But in time I could anticipate what kind of detail he might ask about and then, if it was a refrigerator, answer correctly, "O'Keefe & Merritt!" or as we like to call them, "Oh Grief and Bear It."

Often the games involved wordplay. He would offer up a combination synonym or antonym for a player on the Little League team he coached. "Who is 'Empty Hammer'?" he would ask. Empty Hammer was, of course, Phil Mallot, the pitcher whose house we just delivered three half-gallons and a quart of orange juice to. Sometimes he introduced a word he thought was interesting such as the day he asked me, "What is a pitot tube?" It turned out to be a small tube on the wing of a fighter plane that measured airspeed. He had been a sergeant in the Air Force during World War II stationed in the Pacific where he uncrated and put together P-39 Airacobras and P31 Mustangs less than six months after graduating from high school.

Three years of living in foxholes had made him committed to living in the town he grew up in and having the opportunity to come home for lunch with my mom, which he did every day for thirty-five years until he retired from the dairy. I believe that the word games we played on the milk truck created my interest in analogies and metaphors which later led to an interest in poetry and a degree in creative writing. As a coach I often turned to analogies and metaphors as a way to deal with the challenges I faced on the court. In my third year as head volleyball coach at Nebraska the offense we ran, which was a multiple offense with fakes and options to a quick attacker, was inspired by the creative retreating by the Ogallala Sioux that I read about in Mari Sandoz's *Crazy Horse.*

At some point I began to approach everything as a metaphor for possibilities in coaching volleyball. When collegiate basketball introduced the three-point shot, I found it interesting to see which coaches adapted quickly, understanding not only the impact the three-point shot had on scoring, but the implications for what a successful post player could be. Billy Tubbs at Oklahoma was one of the first to recognize that because of the threat the three-point shot provided, defenses would be more spread out and therefore the ideal post player was not the 7-foot big man who played with his back to the basket but a quicker, smaller, more explosive athlete who could take advantage of the space that was created.

One of the most incredible athletic events I ever saw was the 1988 NCAA Men's Basketball Championship final when Oklahoma, featuring Stacey King and Mookie Blaylock, met Kansas coached by Larry Brown and featuring Danny Manning. The game was so fast that it seemed to be played at warp speed. Both teams had the prototypical player for the type of game they were playing. Kansas had the 6-foot-10-inch Manning who had the body of a small forward and the passing skills of a point guard, and Oklahoma was an offense without a true center but relied on the speed and quickness of its guards and the offensive spacing that allowed the 6-foot-10-inch King to take advantage of his superior quickness and offensive skills. Both teams scored more than fifty points in the first half at a tempo that seemed to favor Oklahoma. Kansas eventually won the game and the national championship, but what was important to me was the observation that both teams were built from the inside out. That is, they were not so much concerned with what they couldn't do as they were in highlighting and emphasizing what they could do with the talent they had. Both coaches seemed to understand what the rule changes could mean to basketball beyond the obvious advantage of scoring three points instead of two.

As I watched the game, I kept asking myself, "How does this apply to coaching volleyball at Nebraska?" There were two principles that seemed to have application. The first was that both coaches understood and exploited the obvious implications of the three-point shot and the not-so-obvious implications and opportunities it created for a different kind of post player. Second, both coaches had recruited players to take advantage of this opportunity. Whether they did this consciously or it just evolved, I don't know. What I do know is that Oklahoma, in particular, would not have been nearly as successful in a system that had not been built on the strength of its athletes. Their defensive pressure created a large percentage of their offense and their guards were effective three-point shooters and passers who created the spacing for Stacey King to be a dominant inside offensive player.

Oklahoma's success was built around exceptional athletes. It was a system that took advantage of their athletic strengths, and it was a system that exploited the advantages of the three-point shot in a way that hadn't been done before. They were ahead of the curve.

What was important in my development as a coach was not so much specific ideas that memorable basketball game gave me, but how I watched it. Because of the early conversations and word games with my father on a milk truck, I had come to appreciate the value in analogies and metaphors. Because my father had installed a curiosity in me about seemingly unimportant details (the name of

13

a refrigerator) he had nurtured a way of gathering information and philosophy that everything may have some potential for giving insight into something else.

My father's emphasis on attention to detail carried over into his coaching in Little League and Babe Ruth League. When practice was rained out other teams went home, but we would go up in the press box and have a skull session on the correct way to put on a pair of baseball pants by turning the pants inside out and blousing them over your game socks. On another day we practiced a type of slide used only in a very specific situation. We had already learned a basic feet-first slide and a hook slide, but on this day he told us that if we ever were beaten by the throw to home plate, rather than slide feet first or try to knock the ball out of the catcher's mitt, we should dive head first to the right side of the baseline then reach out and touch the plate with our hand. He told us that while the odds were still against us, they were considerably better with the catcher trying to tag a sweeping hand rather than an entire torso sliding into the plate.

Several games went by before I found myself rounding third base heading toward home, oblivious to the frantic then disappointed gestures of an 11-year-old third base coach. I saw the Lions Club catcher waiting with the ball in his fat mitt not 10 feet in front of me when I remembered I had an option. Before I knew it, I was diving head first to the right of the catcher then reached out and swatted the plate with my left hand as the umpire shouted an emphatic and delicious "S a a a f e!" The first thing I thought of even before I dusted myself off, even as teammates were running to me with the excitement of winning and the anticipation of free root beer, was preparation.

I was safe because my father had prepared me for a specific situation that did not occur very often and even when it did, the odds for success were not great. After shaking hands with the other team and drinking root beer with my teammates, I sat on the bleachers in the special glow, not just of twilight falling on a Little League baseball diamond in northern Indiana, but in the knowledge that I had achieved a different kind of success that evening. It was not based on athletic talent or luck; it was brought about because someone had thought about the game in a different way.

YOU BEGIN WITH A BOAT

Imagine a boat lying not far offshore. Sitting at one end, with her back to the shore is the coach. She is the only one on the boat who can see clearly where the boat is going. While the twelve rowers, whose backs face their destination cannot see where they are going, they can *feel* when one of their teammates lifts her oar out of the water and the boat begins to change course, almost imperceptibly at first, as the boat begins to turn. If the oar does not return to the water in rhythm with her teammates, the boat will eventually turn in circles.

Is this a group or a team? You can only answer that question if you know where the people in the boat intend to go. A group of people is just that, a group of people. You can find them in restaurants gathered for breakfast or coffee in any town in America. A group only becomes a team when it has a destination, a goal. Having coffee and enjoying each other's company is pleasant, enjoyable, and may even promote the mental health of the people seated at the table, but it is not a team. For it to become a team, it has to have a purpose. Groups can last a long time, even decades. The life of a team is usually much shorter, and it frequently disbands after accomplishing its purpose.

A community forms a committee that becomes a team when it decides to plan, raise funds, and build a swimming pool. The team disbands after the pool is built. A corporation puts together a team to develop a new automobile that initially is just a concept, but moves past ideas to design, engineering, and manufacturing challenges. After the car advances to production, the original design team disbands. The team's purpose is over.

This is one of the paradoxes that a coach of an athletic team faces. The team is artificially kept together within the structure of the educational institution even though the players change on a yearly basis. Teams are formed before they have a purpose. Each athlete may have individual goals or ambitions, but initially there is not the passionate focus on purpose that is there when people are brought together to meet a specific challenge, whether that challenge is finding a cure for SARS disease, reducing our dependence on fossil fuels, or forming a search team to look for a lost hiker.

Athletic teams have all the accoutrements of teams that have been assembled for a passionate purpose. They work hard. They have designated roles. They solve some problems, and if they are lucky they eventually find a place to go that the members are passionate about. But many athletic teams begin rowing before they know where they are trying to go. Much of the time they seem satisfied with whatever destination they happen upon. In other words, they come to define the trip by wherever they land. If they land on the island "Pretty Goodville," that's OK. If they advance to the conference tournament, that's cool. If they make the NCAA tournament, at least they didn't go to some of the other islands, like "NIT" or "the island of losing seasons."

The problem is that it's hard to know where you are going until you have the right talent in the boat. If your purpose is to put out a forest fire, you recruit people who have courage and experience in fighting fires. If you are trying to raise money for the zoo, you can recruit a team comprised of people who like kangaroos and monkeys or you can recruit a team of movers and shakers who have connections in the community to where the real money is. The point is, if you know where you are going, you have a chance to address the real need and recruit the best people to get there.

If a coach recruits the best athletes available, or more accurately, the best "rowers" she can get given the tradition of the program, the academic strength of the school, and the energy and creativity of her staff, she may not know where the team is capable of going until the team has already been at sea for half a season. And this is where many high school and collegiate programs spend their competitive lives, figuring out where they're going with what they've got, until it only begins to emerge each season halfway through the journey.

Is there an easy answer to this? No. Someone once asked me how difficult it is to put together side-out, offensive, and defensive systems in volleyball that leverage the strengths of your best players and hide their deficiencies. I recalled an image I saw years ago near Canyon de Chelly in northwest Arizona. Two Navaho kids were trying to herd seven ponies into a small corral. Several times they got five of the ponies into the corral, but when they turned their attention to the two remaining ponies on the mesa, the original five poured out like coins in a slot machine. That's what it's like when you're trying to build a great system. It's not easy and the result is not perfect. The goal in coaching is not to be perfect but to be better.

There are several challenges that each coach has to confront to build an extraordinary team. You have to recruit as if your professional life depends upon it. It does. Once you have done that (and the commitment to do that is much more important than your perception of who you can recruit and who you can't), then other challenges emerge.

What can the people you have recruited to the boat do or be trained to do at an exceptional level? This is far more important than what they can't do. It will take discipline, creativity, and commitment to leverage the exceptional strengths you have recruited. In time, you may discover that you focus on recruiting people who have the strengths that you coach the best. You learn to leverage those strengths so consistently that you create a brand. You are so distinctive in what you do exceptionally well that even people who don't understand your sport recognize this brand. The goal is to create a team so unique, so consistent in its excellence that it begins to recruit itself. That happens when a recruit watches your team play and sees her own talents matching the talents on the court. The first commandment is "Thou shall recruit with more energy and purpose than you ever thought possible." The second commandment is "Thou shalt leverage that talent into a brand."

Once you have begun these two processes (and they are processes because recruiting and developing your strengths never end), then you can address the next question: Where are we going? Chances are if you are a developing coach or if you are a coach who loves not losing too much or a coach who becomes comfortable with a certain level of success or a coach who is not willing to look foolish . . . the answer to this question is, "not very far."

A few years ago I asked several coaches independently to tell me which head volleyball coaches in Division 1 are "on a journey to win a national championship." Each coach I asked listed the same six people. Some of the coaches they named had already won national championships, but in one case it was obvious to everyone that the head coach of a program that was not yet a top ten program was passionate about building a program would eventually win a national championship. That day came to pass three years later.

There are a couple of interesting observations about the answers of the coaches I polled. First of all, there are 331 Division 1 women's volleyball teams. Yet each coach I questioned listed only six coaches, and they all named the same six.

Does that mean those are the only programs that have the talent, competition, and institutional support to win a national championship? No. In my opinion, the majority of the teams in the Big 10, Big 12, and Pac 10 conferences plus twenty other programs could be on a journey to win a national championship. Does that mean that everyone other than those six coaches is not working hard enough? Hardly. But working hard is different from thinking and dreaming and being passionate about a seemingly unreachable target.

Here's another interesting observation: Only one of the six schools mentioned would have been named if I had asked this question twenty years ago. The perception is that the top teams never change. They do, but sometimes the cycle is longer than our memory. Point in fact: Where were Connecticut men's and women's basketball twenty years ago? Good, maybe, but not challenging for national championships. If someone had told you twenty years ago that Connecticut would be at the nexus of NCAA men's and women's basketball sometime in the future, you probably could have listed twenty other schools that were more likely to emerge.

What happened? The same thing that happens whenever a school that has not been nationally prominent "suddenly" emerges in women's volleyball, gymnastics, football, or softball. There is a fanatical commitment to recruiting talent. There is a coaching staff that has a clear understanding of the combined strengths of the athletes, the institution, and the culture of the local community, and finds creative ways to leverage those strengths. And somewhere along the sideline there is a coach who is willing to take risks; willing to look out over the bow of the boat before she has even recruited the right rowers for the right positions, to look farther across the water than anyone else can see, and say in a voice foolish in its confidence, "The National Championship is where we are going." And she has to continue to say it while passing through waves of injured athletes, lost recruits, disappointing losses, and the perception of others that she is not making headway.

There is nothing so satisfying and rewarding as the coach who chooses to risk as much as she is asking from her athletes, refusing to believe that it will not happen, clearly acknowledging all of the challenges along the way, making herself uncomfortable with her refusal to let go of being great until everything—talent, staff, athletic administration, players, and skeptical fans—are caught up in her wake.

A FOUNDATION FOR COACHING

"The first task of a leader is to keep hope alive." – Joe Battan

Once during a coaching workshop at Creighton University I asked if anyone in the room could tell me what he thought his talent was. One of the points I was hoping to make is my belief that successful people, including successful coaches, have a clear idea of what they do exceptionally well. They know what their talent is and they know how to leverage that talent.

The first person to raise his hand was Bob Warming, head coach of Creighton's men's soccer program. Coach Warming built the soccer program at Creighton from the ground up. He has won conference championships, coached his teams to the NCAA Championship finals, raised funds for a state-of-the-art soccer facility, and is perhaps the most consistently successful coach on the Creighton staff. Without any hesitation, he replied, "I can get kids to do things they don't want to do."

If you aren't a coach you might not understand the complexity of such a simple sentence. In one sentence he not only summed up his unique talent, but the essence of the challenge that faces coaches at every level. Coaching is getting people to believe they can accomplish more than they think they can. Coaching is getting people to want to be better than they think they can be. Coaching is getting people to commit to specific behaviors that give them the best chance to reach the goals they have set with your guidance.

If you don't know Coach Warming, if you don't understand the layers of meaning that come from such a simple response, you might think he believes his talent is manipulating athletes to do things they don't want to do. But that's not what he meant, any more than a great high school math teacher manipulates students to develop an appreciation and application for algebra.

To be sure, great coaches and teachers change the people around them, but they don't do it covertly. They do it by bringing tremendous passion to their work. It's very difficult to be around someone who is passionate about what they are doing without that energy altering the way other people feel about the task at hand.

They do it by witnessing for the things they believe in. They witness for their values. They witness for how they believe the game should be played. They witness for the non-negotiable behaviors that are the backbone to every great team. Ultimately, they witness to the belief that the people they are coaching have *the right stuff to get the job done*. All great coaching and teaching is built on a DNA of hopefulness: the belief that if we commit to certain behaviors, if we work with enthusiasm and focus, if we care more for the mission of the team than our unwillingness to be uncomfortable, then great things will happen.

This is the keystone that my coaching philosophy is built on. It is a philosophy that has grown out of years of observing patterns that consistently emerge with exceptional teaching and coaching. It is not what I think great coaching should be. It is not what I have read exceptional coaching should be. It is what I have witnessed whenever a group of talented individuals under the shepherding of an exceptional coach has moved beyond random focus and success to become a great team.

POETRY, PURPOSE, AND COACHING

I believe that anything worth doing with passion begins with a vision. In the beginning my vision was defined by a fear for survival: *Please let me do this well enough that I get the opportunity to do it for another year.* After a few years with some success, I began to ask myself what the purpose of Nebraska Volleyball was beyond winning volleyball matches, and what my role was in bringing it about. My first purpose statement was written in 1980:

I would like to create an environment for Nebraska Volleyball where extraordinary female athletes have the opportunity to compete with such athleticism and grace that if another exceptional athlete walked into the Coliseum she would want to join them.

The statement is as interesting for what it doesn't say as what it says. It does not mention wins and losses. It does not mention conference or national championships. It does not mention All-American certificates or academic achievements. It is not a statement of goals, but rather a statement of the spirit that I hoped to create, and as evidenced by the last part of the sentence, it was almost evangelical in its intent.

Where did this vision come from? I'm not sure. I think it emerged out of my imagination and memory about what it might *feel* like to be a part of something that was equal parts communion, performance, joy, and grace. Whenever I go back and read that purpose statement, I am reminded of the lines that end William Butler Yeats' poem, *Among School Children:*

> *O body swayed to music, O brightening glance,*
> *How can we know the dancer from the dance?*

23

Was I thinking of those lines when I wrote the first purpose statement for Nebraska Volleyball? Not consciously. But I had taught the poem as an English professor at Louisburg College and poetry was a large of part of my life, having earned an M.F.A. in the Creative Writing Workshop from the University of Arkansas. The lines remind me that throughout my own life I have had a tendency to be apart from things, relying on analytical skills when I longed to let go and be a part of the dance. I didn't want Nebraska Volleyball to be apart from things. I wanted it to be a culture where something important happened, and when people came to watch, they would be a part of it, too.

Maybe this question is even more important. Why would a developing coach write down a vision that did not include specific goals? We *did* set goals, both individually and as a team, but I think the absence of them in a purpose statement indicates that even before Nebraska Volleyball achieved significance on a national stage, I sensed that there would have to be something beyond championships to make this meaningful for me and the people who would be a part of it.

Some people are surprised when they learn of my background in poetry; they see it as a strange curriculum in the education of a coach. I cannot imagine any field of study that would have prepared me more for coaching. Why?

Poetry is made up of patterns: patterns in rhythm, word choice, line length, emphasis, story, and metaphor. The patterns a writer chooses become in a sense his court, and the rules that he plays by. Robert Frost once said that "writing poetry without rhyme is like playing tennis without a net." While I may prefer the softer lob shots of assonance and half rhymes, I understand what he meant. Games, *and both writing poetry and playing volleyball are games,* are more interesting if there are imposed limitations. For Frost, the limitations were writing iambic verse with a specific rhyme scheme. For a volleyball player, the limitations are the net, the rules of the game, and the dimensions of the court.

Coaching is about patterns as well. Volleyball is a game of tempo and rhythm. There is the tempo of the referee's whistle and how quickly the middle attacker shuttles the ball to a teammate waiting to serve. There is the rhythm and deliberate approach of a dynamic outside attacker and the lighter footwork of a quick middle. There are a hundred different ways to close the block, and each of them would sound different on a keyboard. There is the pursuit of a middle back defender and the ballet of letting go in a drop-step passer.

There are tactical patterns as well. Serving short can create the illusion that time has stopped and move the opposing setter into the left side of her brain. Which tempo will make our opponent uncomfortable? With which player does the opposing coach have the least patience and how can we disrupt her rhythm? How does the opposing coach solve problems? Are there patterns to her decisions following time-outs?

There are endgames in both poetry and athletic competition. How does a poet solve the problem of ending the poem? Sometimes with the introduction of repetition, as in the last stanza of Frost's *Stopping By A Woods on A Snow Evening:*

> The woods are lovely, dark and deep.
> But I have promises to keep,
> And miles to go before I sleep,
> And miles to go before I sleep.

Sometimes a writer signals the end of a poem with a twist in meaning suggested by a change in the level of language. That is what I attempted in a poem that appears to be about fly-fishing, but introduces another possibility in the last line.

Trust and the River

> I've come
> to a place where the river bends,
> like an opposable thumb,
> that allows me to attach
> this elegant elk hair caddis
> to the tippet with a knot
> I once knew the name of.

Despite the sunlight fading
with the falling sky
the caddis rise,
and risk everything
to become like stars.

There is no certainty
the dark shadow
lying beneath
the riffle will lift
to my presentation
which hovers above the river,
a forgotten language.

Finally,
beneath the tumbling grace
of cool rushing water
the long shadow rises,
Zeppelin like, beneath
the spent hackle,
and I feel my lungs
filling with oxygen and joy . . .

But something isn't right,
and centuries of being wild,
hidden and beautiful
urge the big rainbow back
beneath the scree-covered ledge.

It is easier to love than to trust.

Moving from the descriptive language of fly-fishing to a philosophical statement about trust and love not only lets the reader know the poem is coming to a conclusion, but that the preceding lines may be about more than just fly-fishing. As one of my writer friends once said, *"There's a woman in there somewhere."*

26

Endgame in volleyball is about innovation and adaptation as well. It is like jazz where a musician improvises off the pre-existing patterns established earlier in the song. In game three you chose to have your team serve short to take away the rhythm of the slide, but in endgame your best server is pinning the right hip of the receiver in zone 1 to the sideline. Your setter tipped the ball behind her head for a point in game four and now as she is hovering above the net with a committed block shadowing her potential attack, she releases the ball to the pin with a slightly quicker tempo.

Before I digressed with poetry and endgame I was talking about an early sense of purpose with Nebraska Volleyball. Goals are measurable. Purpose is not. How could you possibly know whether or not a talented young girl would want to join the players on the court when she entered the Coliseum for the first time? You would have to ask each girl as she watched the players swaying to the music of the game, the pep band, the rhythms of attack and defend, the heartbeat of a teammate calling for the ball, exhorting each other in an unscripted dance of talent and passion. But if you have been to the Nebraska Coliseum to watch a volleyball match you would know, and you would not need to ask.

Another wonderful application from poetry to purpose is the use of metaphor. When we make didactic statements of fact we are using the left side of our brain. When we introduce the comparisons in the form of metaphor, we move to the right side of our brain, which has the potential for more creativity.

To say that Joe DiMaggio was graceful and athletic is a statement of fact. To call him the "Yankee Clipper" is an open-ended metaphor that moves us to picture a clipper ship sailing effortlessly yet purposefully through the center field of Yankee Stadium. To tell an outsider hitter to get into extension, with a three-step approach, fire her hips followed by her shoulder and finally her wrist is instruction. Telling an attacker to get "big" asks her not to think about what she is doing but to feel it.

Volleyball is a game that is best played with intuitive intelligence. There is not enough time to analytically think your way through every execution and fundamental. From my experience, you cannot think your way through the process of writing a poem any more than a setter can think her way through the geometry of a back set.

Writing poetry is like playing a game. To write well requires preparation, experience, and mentoring, but ultimately it is a dance where we are open to steps we haven't yet imagined. When creativity happens on the volleyball court with grace and serendipitous joy, it is impossible to know the difference between the player and the game, the dancer and the dance.

THE DEVELOPMENT OF THE EXTRAORDINARY COACH

I believe there are several distinct phases to a coach's life. This observation is not the result of university-sponsored research, but anecdotal evidence that emerged as I had time to reflect during the hours spent lying in bad motel rooms while waiting to leave for equally bad pre-match meals.

The *beginning volleyball coach* is frequently a former player if she is female, and almost always a failed basketball player if he is male. The female has an advantage in that she has played organized volleyball with the attendant coaches, managers, kneepads, and fifteen-passenger vans. The beginning male coach is wagging with passion for a sport that he can play with some success without being dominated by the size and fast-twitch muscles that are found in revenue sports.

Passion is a beginning coach's greatest ally. People choose to become coaches for one of two reasons: They genuinely enjoy the game or because a coach has impacted their life.

The beginning coach's crucible is that *she doesn't know what she doesn't know.* Unless she has a parent who coaches, a beginning coach is only vaguely aware that coaching involves more than what takes place on the practice floor. Motivating, marketing, recruiting, witnessing, scheduling, teaching, selling candy bars, negotiating, system-building, and driving unsafe vehicles are part of the iceberg that lies below the beginning coach's awareness. Ah, but the passion. To be a beginning coach is not about age or the number of years you have coached, it is about being so excited to be a part of a game you love that you sometimes put your pants on backward.

The *developing coach* is perhaps the most critical phase in a coaching life. The developing coach is experienced enough to know what she doesn't know, and may even lie awake at night wondering when everyone else is going to figure out that she doesn't know what she is doing. She is motivated by fear—fear of losing, fear of not winning enough, fear of not being paid what the women's basketball coach is paid, fear of not landing a great recruit or persuading the best athlete in school to give up soccer for volleyball.

The developing coach is at a crossroads that can last for a year or two, or for the rest of her professional life. She has attended camps and clinics run by successful peers. She may have been an assistant coach for a well-respected coach, and she has read everything she can about coaching and implementing a perimeter defense. She has been intentional in her own development. What remains is for her to develop insight into her own talent and mindset. She knows more about a rotation defense than her natural strengths. She knows more about footwork patterns than why she is such a poor communicator during time-outs. She may spend years trying to coach like her own high school or collegiate coach before she realizes she needs to find her own path.

To continue to grow, the developing coach must make a commitment to learn more about herself. What do I do well? Where am I limited? How can I surround myself with people who have talents and skills to complement my own? How can I move toward collaborative leadership? This is not an easy process, and it can be helpful to have a mentor or coaching friends you trust who can help you come to your own truth.

In time, the developing coach may discover what she can do extraordinarily well and develop systems and philosophies of coaching that leverage her talent. If she doesn't do this work, she stalls. Each season ends with the coach making the same mistakes while blaming the lack of progress on things she perceives beyond her control.

The *master coach* is defined not by the level at which she is coaching, but by the action she takes to leverage her strengths. While master coaches are rare, they are just as likely to be found in a high school gym as in an NCAA Division I arena.

The master coach, while competent in most areas of coaching, is extraordinary in one or two. She may be an expert in tempo or training fundamentals or working with learning-disabled kids. She may be great at introducing discipline to the entitled children of suburban millionaires. She may be extraordinary at building confidence or building a community of trust. She may be able to teach a goose to pass perfect balls from zone 1.

She doesn't ignore the things that she isn't great at. She collaborates with her team and assistant coaches who have natural talents in areas other than her own, and she gives them the opportunity to experiment, fail, and succeed.

The crucible for the master coach is change. When a coach has experienced a high level of success for an extended time period, she may not recognize when adjustments need to be made. A master coach can come to believe that the key to her success is *the system,* the established patterns that worked in the past, and she may not be open to a changing game and culture.

She may blame rally score, the libero, fifteen subs, foreign athletes, and text messaging as reasons her program is slipping and not recognize she has lost her passion for recruiting talent.

The crucible the master coach faces is that because of her program's success, she is vulnerable to becoming too comfortable. And comfortable in coaching is similar to rolling a die in the game of "Chutes and Ladders" and finding yourself on a quick trip back to the beginning, landing on your butt not knowing what you don't know.

THE DIFFERENCE BETWEEN TALENT AND SKILL

If you had the choice between recruiting someone for the setter position who has great hands and average foot speed or another person with great feet and undeveloped hands, which would you choose? The answer to this question depends on several variables, not the least of which is your prowess at training setters and how soon the recruit has to be on the court.

If I were running a school for coaches, the one thing I would want every graduate to have insight into is the difference between talent and skill. Both are necessary to be successful, but over time, a talent-based program has the potential to build championships. A program that relies primarily on skill can be consistently good, but rarely develops into something extraordinary.

For the sake of my argument, let's define a skill as something that we can teach someone to do. It is not primarily dependent upon whether the student is age 15 or 50 as long as they have the mental capacity to understand what we are asking them to do and the physical development to accomplish the task.

Erasing a blackboard is a skill. Answering the phone politely is a skill. Arithmetic is a skill. So is spelling (a skill that I have chosen not to develop). I believe that learning to set a volleyball is primarily a skill. I think almost any healthy person with hands that can surround an iPod can be trained to set a volleyball in less than three weeks.

But getting to a volleyball in a balanced position before it hits the floor off an errant pass is a talent. Having a sense of where you are on the court is a talent. Fast-twitch muscles and an imagination that allows the setter to see where her attackers are approaching behind her is a talent.

Skills are patterns that can be learned. Talents are by-products of our genetic makeup. Size is a talent. Quickness is talent. Vision is talent. Having a kinesthetic awareness of what your body is doing is a talent. The willingness to both lead and serve your fellow players is a talent. Passing a tough floating serve is a talent.

Whoa, what did I just say, and what does it imply? Serve reception can be improved, especially at an early age. But the ability to track the ball, the ability to triangulate and move to the right spot before the ball arrives, is primarily based on God-given talents that are refined with good training and experience.

I base this on the anecdotal evidence of twenty-six years of coaching, some of them spent trying to get slow-footed but trained volleyball players to move their feet before they moved their shoulders in response to a short serve.

I once asked Sue Woodstra, who in the late 1970s played on the U.S. National team and at the time was quite possibly the best passer in the Milky Way, how long it took her to develop her unique ability. She responded by saying that she could do it almost from the first time she walked onto the court. She got better with repetition and training, but her hand-eye coordination and touch on the ball was uniquely hers in the same way that Etta James is inimitable when she belts out *At Last*.

I have never seen a volleyball player enter college and develop into a great outside hitter who didn't already have a strong shoulder rotation. It would be easier to teach a cat to play "Scrabble" than to teach someone who can't throw to develop arm speed after age 16. Basketball coaches tell me the same thing about shooting. A good shooter entering college can get better, but a poor shooter can't be trained to be great.

We can improve the efficiency of a player's footwork. We can teach her how to communicate and how to seal the block. We cannot teach her to be tall. We will have great difficulty teaching her to be competitive if she has grown up in a culture that was not goal-oriented.

Of course, I am overstating my case. But not by as much as you might think. I believe that training skills is critical to the success of a team, but leveraging individual players' innate talents is the step that moves good teams to become extraordinary teams.

We need to broaden our vision of what talent is. Being inclusive is a talent. Caring about your teammates is a talent. The willingness to be uncomfortable as you work to learn or refine a new skill is a talent.

Great teams are made from coaches figuring out how to take the talents of their players and make them the focal point of the team. Talent is transferable and it is consistent. If you don't believe me, watch the cat come running into the kitchen when the light in the refrigerator goes on.

ROAD TRIPS

Journal Entry: September 28, 1988

The only thing predictable about a road trip is that the upperclassmen will ride in the van with the assistant coach and the freshmen will be banned to the van with the head coach. This seems to be the pattern at almost every school throughout the country.

The head coach talks about academics, talks about volleyball, talks about past players, talks about what this team has to do to reach its potential. What's worse, he just doesn't talk, he asks questions. He asks, "Sue, what is the most difficult adjustment you've had to make coming to Nebraska?" Sue has only been at Nebraska for four weeks and to her knowledge, she hasn't had to make any adjustments, but she has been warned by the upperclassmen and so she has an answer. "Well, I guess it would be that everything is so much more disciplined here than it was in high school. I mean, there's a reason for everything we do." This answer will not keep the head coach from asking more questions, but it may slow him down while he considers such a thoughtful answer from a freshman.

Meanwhile, the other van is rocking. Everyone, including the assistant coach, is wearing headphones. Nine heads are moving up and down to various rhythms while behind the seat a bag of M&Ms is passed from player to player as deftly as an off-speed shot to the corner. The van itself seems to take on a rhythm as it bounces up and down using a generous amount of highway, sometimes trailing the head coach's van by 6 feet, sometimes by a mile and a half.

As the players see it, the only advantage to being in the head coach's van is that the decision on where the team will eat is made in that vehicle. But even then, the players will have little input as the head coach stops his dissertation on spiker coverage to announce, "OK, what's it going to be, Souper Salad or Spaghetti Works?"

THE INTEGRATED COACH

"The task in becoming a leader is to become an integrated person." – Warren Bennis

There are buzzwords in leadership and coaching. "Mission" is one. It is used so often in so many different ways it has lost its power to engage us like it once did.

"Integrated" is another buzzword in leadership. I like the concept but until I heard a speaker who had recovered from cancer with the help of a team of health professionals, I didn't have a clear picture for everything the word implies.

This was a powerful speaker who related how she dealt with the challenge of breast cancer by working with an *integrated* team comprised of an oncologist, a nutritionist, nurses, a massage therapist, clergy, and others who "talked with each other" about the best way to help Lynette meet and defeat a disease that was aggressively attacking her body. It was a holistic approach in which each of the professionals involved not only knew of the other professionals' roles, but embraced the idea that Lynette had a better chance for recovery because all of the dimensions of her personality and her physical, mental, and spiritual health were being addressed.

As Lynette told her story I came to understand that an integrated person is someone whose talents, skills, and values *talk to each other.* The first image that came to mind was that of a Swiss Army knife in which several tools are housed, some of which we frequently use (the big blade and the scissors), some of which we find interesting even if we don't use them very often (the saw and toothpick), and a couple of which we're not even sure what they do (like undeveloped talents).

Imagine a leadership tool that houses all of your talents and skills. You can unfold talents like your natural ability to communicate, to be inclusive, to push teammates to exceptional performance. You can also engage the skills you've developed to organize an effective meeting, to memorize and learn information about team members' families, to run an effective practice, or write a business letter.

But this image is too static, too two-dimensional to provide the best metaphor for leadership. Imagine a leadership tool in four dimensions where the talents and skills of the leader are in constant relationship with each other. They are continually talking with each other so that if you unfold any talent or skill, other complementary talents and skills are engaged as well.

If you open your innate competitiveness (a talent), other talents and skills that are enhanced by this specific talent open up as well (such as your talent for solving problems and the skill you learned and developed for active listening).

The best coaches and leaders do not necessarily have more talents and skills than other people who are merely "good" leaders. What sets them apart is that their talents are constantly talking to each other. They have the ability to engage all of their resources (talents and skills) to work together to attack a problem in a creative and effective way. Their talents are collaborative.

It's like a surgeon sending small lasers of energy from every angle that meet at a tumor to combine and form a whole that is greater than the sum of the parts without destroying the healthy tissue surrounding the tumor. It means that great leaders are always using their talents in relationship with other talents and skills to address the challenge at hand.

To do this they need a clear understanding of what their talents are. Unfortunately, many people are not only unaware of what their talents are, they frequently assume they have a specific talent in abundance while their teammates would clearly disagree. (The person who sings the loudest in the pew is not necessarily the most talented voice.) And so there are basketball coaches who choose to have their team press without quickness. There are volleyball coaches who pass with three players when only two have depth perception. There are ineffective shooters taking the last shot of the game. There are middle blockers without "soft eyes" and quarterbacks running the option without the ability to read on the run.

On the other hand, when you leave a competition feeling that you should have won but didn't, and the other team didn't appear to be as talented, there is a very good chance you lost to an integrated coach who was able to leverage his team's talent and skill in a way that everything was working toward the same purpose. This is how a pelican (despite looking like a rabbit backing up) is able to fly quite well. This is why you sometimes find a rat snake living in a birdhouse.

This is why great coaches have a four-dimensional leadership tool located in their brain that allows them to leverage the talents of over-achieving players into an extraordinary team.

ADAPTATION AND NEUROSIS

We have a Maine Coon cat named Sara who has some noteworthy behaviors. She loves water, which we learned only after unsuccessfully trying to keep her off the kitchen table by using a squirt bottle, and she is passionate about fetching a small rubber ball and then placing it in our laps.

She loves to fetch so much that she introduced an innovation to the game. After retrieving the ball she takes it to the top of the basement stairs, drops it, watches it fall antiphonally down the stairs, then pounces on it and carries it back up to the couch where she drops it, ever so indifferently, into our laps. It is as if we weren't challenging her enough by just throwing the ball into the next room. She is extending endgame.

Recently she adopted a new behavior that is not as endearing. She spends endless hours hunkered down on the kitchen floor peering into the darkness beneath the refrigerator. A few weeks ago, with the coming of winter, she found a field mouse that she shepherded around the house until the mouse died of anxiety, stress, and a loss of hope.

I suspect that she first spied the mouse at the base of the refrigerator and therefore assumes that at any moment another mouse may appear. She is camped out at the base of the refrigerator 24/7. There is no thought of retrieving a ball, perching on the kitchen table, playing with water, or walking over the keys of the laptop while I'm e-mailing a friend. She is one committed Maine Coon.

If there was a cat psychologist we could send Sara to he might say the following to her, "There may be another mouse living under the refrigerator, but even if there is, you need to get on with your life." Or he might suggest that the game has changed, and say something like this: "Sara, one of the most critical things in life is adaptation. It is time to come to terms with the fact that sometimes under stress our inclination is to do the same thing over and over again with more intensity and expect a different result. You have replaced curiosity with neurosis."

And so, dear reader, I place this ball in your lap. When we see a coach who was once consistently successful begin to string together seasons that are not up to his standards, it may be because he is hunkered down staring into the darkness of what worked in the past and cannot bring himself to give it up.

Consider the changes in recent years that call for innovation and adaptation: the introduction of rally score and the libero; coaching "Millennials," – an entire generation that has never filled its own water bottle; watching your team disintegrate on You Tube; bladderless volleyballs, swing blocking; the lack of a draft; Penn State into the Big 10 and Hawaii cut adrift; the best athletes moving from the middle to the left; junior programs encouraging former players to become free agents; the rise and demise of ankle supports; texting from the bench; more laptops than conversations; rotation, perimeter, and flex defenses evolving to homeostasis; everyone throwing the ball to zone 1; run-throughs becoming none-throughs; more ivory-billed woodpecker sightings than middles in transition; coaches with buyouts; vanishing Russian leapers and emerging Russian right sides; and where in the world is Sid Feldman?

Sometimes we just run out of gas. Unless you're a coyote, it's hard to keep adapting. It is easier just to lie down on the gymnasium floor and stare into the darkness and pretend that what worked before we invaded Iraq and ignored the Kyoto Treaty will work today if we just do it with more intensity, even as the Arctic is melting.

I admire all coaches. But the ones I admire most are the few who had it going, lost it for a while, and got it back. UCLA coach Andy Banachowski comes to mind, and Carolyn Condit at Miami, Joe Paterno,

Al Gore and that ditzy lady on "Desperate Housewives." It takes tremendous courage to reinvent yourself or your coaching philosophy. It requires a reality check and an unwillingness to see yourself as a victim. Most of all it requires energy, which falls through the hourglass of a coaching life faster than the changes it tries to confront. It requires self-reflection and the courage to listen to a good friend or mentor who can tell you the truth.

Experience is only an advantage if we are willing to reflect and examine the experiences we have. At the end of a tough season we need to sift through the debris and see if any patterns emerge: ineffective communication, a lack of collaborative coaching, indifferent recruiting, or a tendency to have wrong people in the wrong position. Are we committed to adaptation or being comfortable with a vision that is outdated?

I love our cat, but if she doesn't recognize that the base of the refrigerator is not the sun and come up with a different plan, we're going to change her name to something embarrassing for a Maine Coon, supposedly the most adaptive of all cats, to something like "Fluffy" or "Rummy." That should do it.

THE COYOTE COACH

We live on a bluff above an oxbow in Fossil Creek, looking west toward Longs Peak, the Indian Peaks, and the rest of Colorado's Front Range. On the far side of the creek are native grasses and thickets that are home to prairie dogs, rattlesnakes, bald eagles, hawks, voles, and coyotes.

Until today, I had only heard the coyotes when they returned from hunting late at night. They yipped and howled almost every night through the winter, their barks as crisp and sharp as if they were only a few yards away. The neighbors next door, a pilot and a physician, were so concerned that they reinforced the locks on their newborn's windows.

This morning I discovered the coyotes actually are less than a football field away. Their den is in a bramble of plum bushes just above the creek and my wife, Anne, spotted them as they returned in the early morning after their hunt. They are hard to see, even when you know where they are, because their fur is the exact color and texture of the prairie grasses they move through.

The best way to describe how they move is to make "alert" an active verb. They are constantly in the now, taking in information about their changing environment with every flare of the nostrils, every paw they lift to the prairie, and every shadow or particle of light that is different from their last breath.

These are not the emaciated coyotes as depicted by Wile E. Coyote in the Road Runner cartoons. They do not so much slink as consider their options. In real life, you would lose a lot of money betting on roadrunners, mice, rabbits, or cats out for a short walk. Coyotes own a much healthier vigorish than the bookies in Vegas. They are the most successful predators in North America. There are significantly more coyotes today than there were a century ago, something that's not true for bears, mountain lions, wolverines, owls, and wolves.

Their territory has moved from primarily the arid Southwest to Midwestern backyards and park lands in the East. They can be found thriving in every major city in the country, and there is a very good chance that if you are reading this in any state but Hawaii there is a coyote within a cab ride.

Despite organized attempts by wildlife officials and spontaneous Saturday morning hunts with dogs, noisemakers and shotguns, coyotes continue to thrive and expand their homeland exponentially. They can survive on voles or Twinkies, garbage or rib eyes. They can scavenge or hunt. They hunt alone or in groups. They can communicate that food is contaminated, and they don't make the same mistake twice.

This last observation is why I admire them so much. While humans tend to notice similarities in their environment, coyotes focus on the differences. If a rock is in the path that wasn't there yesterday, they choose a different path. If a shadow appears above a ridge that wasn't there before, a coyote's amygdala is on notice. Every decision is a survival decision. They do not let sentimentality, habits, or last year's way of doing things get in the way. A coyote's point of view is something that an experienced coach could benefit from.

We all know successful coaches who have a blind spot created by their own success. Sometimes their training has not kept up with technical changes. Sometimes they have relied so much on a particular talent (say, work ethic) that they don't realize they have not developed a coaching skill in another area, such as collaborative leadership.

Some coaches spend more time complaining about Generation Y than they do in researching the strengths of the millennial generation and developing a plan on how to coach them. Some coaches are so consumed with rule changes they don't support, they don't figure out how to take advantage of the implications of a twenty-five-point game with liberal officiating. Some coaches who value stability and family fail to see the impact when their last three recruits are transfers.

Coyotes would not make these mistakes. They cannot afford to because they would not be alive the next day to make another one. But coaches in established programs can fail to see the impact of habits that are no longer successful because talent can delay the impact of neurotic coaching.

The best way for a coach to become like a coyote is to have frequent contact with a mentor or peer group who cares about his or her development and has been invited to share honest observations. This can be a former coach, a counselor, a spouse, or a coach from a different sport. It helps if the person has some insight into the sport you coach, but what a mentor really needs is the ability to see the issues in your blind spot.

Great presidents have had mentors, as have generals, poets, and NASCAR drivers. To reach our full potential we need a coyote coach or two who is willing to tell us the truth about the rock in the path or the shadows that loom above the ridge. It's time to call one up out of the plum bushes.

COACHING IS HARD

Coaching is hard, but we already know that. So why do we get so angry when we are continually presented with challenges that by definition go with the job? We get angry because once every few years our biorhythms align with the moon and we somehow are graced with a team that comes together and exceeds our expectations, is well groomed, does not rob convenience stores, uses birth control, and gets back to base position. We are duped into thinking that coaching is not supposed to be difficult.

On some level we know that the DNA of coaching is adaptation and innovation. My favorite mantra to the right-side blocker who keeps watching the ball instead of the attacker is, "Please take charge of this. Give me a new problem to solve. If you keep this up you're going to end up wearing a baseball cap the rest of your life." (We have her wear the cap to discourage her from watching the ball.)

How many times have you had a "eureka" moment during practice followed by the observation, "I knew that." Why do we forget what we already know? Why do we forget that our setter loses tempo when she does not get to her front foot? Why do we forget that our outside hitter has a better chance of getting into graduate school at Yale than in getting to a release position on a backcourt attack? Why do we forget to remind the assistant coach not to book the team at Chuck and Jim's Motor Inn in Manhattan, Kansas? Why is the assistant coach more consistent with his hair gel than with monitoring weight training?

Maybe the hardest thing about this profession is that while the talent keeps changing, the challenges are all too familiar. See if at least a few of these don't happen almost every year:

1. You lose at least one starter to a knee injury, ankle sprain, bird flu, first love, or terminal acne.
2. Your conference rival filled a hole in the lineup with a player from Uzbekistan. She has a Hertz logo on her left sleeve.
3. A freshman who committed to you when she was 12 is not the person you thought she was. At least you didn't think she was more interested in freeing Tibet and wearing a blanket to class than she was in becoming your starting libero.
4. Two players cry on each other's shoulder in the locker room after every practice because they respond to "key words" from the head coach as if she were handing out live grenades.
5. Halfway through the season the volunteer assistant "loses interest" in videotape exchange and begins to take interest in the third middle blocker.
6. The Salt Water Flats University Classic turns out to have three teams instead of four.
7. Your team has beaten USC, Florida, and Washington, and that Pablo guy has you rated 126.
8. On the one night the athletic director decides to come to the game your manager substitutes the Red Hot Chili Peppers' explicit version of the national anthem.
9. Because the football team loses its fifth game in a row, resulting in a drop in home attendance, your team travels to the conference tournament in the ticket manager's Winnebago.
10. Someone on the tournament NCAA selection committee misinterprets the guidelines and values cumulative reception errors over head-to-head competition, resulting in your team doing some early Christmas shopping.

If none of these things happened to you this year, congratulations. Sit down, relax, and open a bottle of pinot noir. You are about to win the national championship.

HOW COACHES GET INTO TROUBLE

Several years ago a coach contacted me about helping her improve her bench coaching. This was a coach I knew well and had even coached against. She had built a successful program, recruited talented athletes, and won conference titles. She was concerned because while she felt that she was a good recruiter and trainer, she didn't consider herself a very good game coach.

She asked if I would work with her on game coaching issues, so I arranged times to see her team practice and watch her coach in game situations. Three weeks later I was watching her run a light practice the day before her school would host an early season tournament.

Nothing out of the ordinary happened in practice except a brief interaction in the middle of a coach-controlled scrimmage. The first team was supposed to side-out three times in a row before they would move on to the next rotation. The setter had been instructed to set two of the three eligible front-row attackers because these two players needed to become more comfortable with running specific plays.

The second unit, comprised of four players (some of whom thought they should be on the other side of the net) plus two assistant coaches, knew which plays the first unit was trying to run. Frequently they were there waiting with a big block that made it difficult for the first team to succeed.

Two backcourt specialists were teeing off with jump serves and because there was little pressure on them, they were serving much tougher than they did in matches. The first unit was having difficulty siding out one time, let alone three times in a row. With each unsuccessful attempt, the veins on the head coach's neck grew more pronounced until her entire body took on the furrowed texture of a Van Gogh painting.

At last the magma rose in the head coach's posture and she called for a water break and confronted the team's setter. She couldn't yell at the assistant coach because the head coach had designed the drill. She couldn't yell at the second team for playing with abandon because they knew the play. She couldn't yell at the players serving tougher than they ever would in a match because that's what she asked them to do.

So she challenged the only person she could, the setter. She challenged her set selection. She challenged her location. She challenged why she chose to make everything so difficult. The truth was (and deep down the coach probably knew it) the drill was stacked against the first team and it wasn't the setter's fault. The coach was reacting to her own needs and she was angry about not designing a better drill.

This happens a lot more than you think it would, and *it happens because the coach loses sight of the real need.* The real need is for the team to be successful and develop confidence in their ability to side-out in each rotation. If the real need was to develop mental toughness or work through the unfairness of sport, then it might be a great drill. But on the day before a match, that was not the issue the coach was addressing.

She would have been better off with players blocking instead of the assistant coaches. She would have been better off with someone serving a slow top-spin serve alternating with the jump servers. She would have been better off not telling the second unit what options the first unit was working on. She may have come to understand these things as a bad drill unfolded, but she compounded bad planning with stubbornness, and stayed with a drill that worked against the real need.

The moral is this: When you realize you've created a drill that doesn't address the real need, get out of it as soon as you can, gracefully if possible, but if not, call for a water break or have the manager hit the fire alarm. Nothing is worse than staying in a drill that creates confusion or undermines an attempt to build confidence.

AFTER THE LOSS

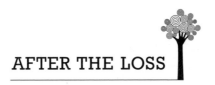

They consider my voice
An inappropriate companion
To the pounding of their blood,
Hot with fatigue and disappointment.

Their heads are bent
Like a ficus toward light,
But there is no light.
Instead they wait
For the practiced words
That huddle in my brain,
Pocket change from losing.

And I know that I cannot reach
Them with words.

And so we breathe in silence,
A conspiracy of players and coaches
Reassured by rhythmic heaving
Of spent muscle, flesh and synapse.

Each letting go reminds us:

We were prepared.
  There was opportunity.
    We could have won.

These unspoken truths are
What we take with us.
That, and this solitude,
This beautiful, tired breathing.

WHY I LOVE GREAT SETTERS

"Poets are the shepherds of our being." – G.W.F. Hegel

If Hegel had been born two centuries later and had a daughter who played the setter position, he might have said, "Setters are the shepherds of our game." Coaches are supposed to value one position as much as another in the same way that a general embraces an artilleryman, a cook, and a tank commander. If that's the case, then take away my stars and epaulets and let me take my last grenade surrounded by setters.

Why do I feel this way when women's volleyball is becoming more like the men's game in which the role of the setter has been reduced to setting hittable balls to the outside, not being used by the opponent's left-side attacker, and setting a quick attacker in transition when a perfect dig coincides with a Cubs pennant?

If I were cynical I might conclude that the era of the great setter has passed, but I love setters too much to not believe that some day middle attackers will again fly around the court attacking from geometries and tempos that a starfighter would envy, and an equally talented setter will deliver the ball from 15 feet off the net.

The lack of imagination in certain tents of contemporary volleyball is not why I love setters. I love them because by the very definition of their name, they are a testimony to servant leadership. Keep in mind that a great servant leader can kick you in the butt when the situation calls for it.

I love setters because if you have made the right choice, you get to coach someone who is not self-absorbed or a compulsive perfectionist. If your setter needs counseling and constant reassurance, you chose the wrong door. If she asks "why?" more than "how?" you'd better keep looking.

Setters have to make hundreds of decisions in a volleyball match. The other players—middle blockers, outside hitters, libero, the substitutes playing grab-ass at the end of the bench—while important, primarily react to the ball. The setter, as President George W. Bush put it, is the *decider*. It is the difference between riding in a kiddy car at an amusement park and driving a Porsche.

How much judgment does it take to play middle back in a gold-medal-squared defense where you could nail your left shoe to the floor and be *in position*? How much judgment does it take for a 6-foot-4-inch trained ace attacker who can touch 10 feet, 6 inches to fire her right hip, contract her abs and whip her arm through a piece of Korean leather? How much judgment does it take for the serving specialist (translation: the outside hitter who didn't pan out) to decide to serve to zone 1 after the hyperactive first assistant flashes a signal with pointer finger fourteen times, occasionally on the wrong side of a clipboard?

I love setters because they get to make the decisions that determine whether their team will be in position to win. I love setters because the best ones do not make these decisions based on their own priorities or goals. They do not make decisions based on their most comfortable set or whether they liked the pre-game meal at the crappy motel with the same sentimental picture of a faded red barn leaning into the wind in every hallway.

I love great setters because they do not make decisions based on their wannabe boyfriend's panic attacks when they are on the road. I love great setters because all of their decisions are held to one compass when they are on the court: Will this decision give my team the best chance to compete? And they make that decision in a millisecond, a hundred times each match.

The decisions that don't work out they learn from, and move on to the next decision unless they have a wag for a coach who has little insight into the position, and who does not understand that trust and rhythm are more important than the coach's own anxiety, and so he challenges them in a time-out because of a trap set (an error in execution, not of judgment) that happened six plays ago.

I think that some coaches aren't sure about what to look for when choosing someone to train in the setter position. Head, feet, posture, and hands are the most important elements, in that order. Hands can be trained. Posture can be learned. Even a lack of quickness can be improved by recognizing that *the most important thing is not how fast the setter gets to the ball, but how balanced she is when she arrives.*

This is accomplished by training her to not leave her base position at the net before she knows where the ball is going, and by learning to take small steps as she pads quickly to the ball. Long strides are for drum majors and picking up splits at the bowling alley. Balance is oxygen for a setter.

Even how a setter thinks and processes decisions can be greatly improved with training. Having said that, give me a setter who comes from a family that looks each other in the eye when they talk; someone who has had a part-time job; someone who isn't afraid of competition and understands that courage is choosing to act with confidence even when there is evidence that the opponent or the circumstances are overwhelming; someone who instinctively knows who to bark at and who to hug; someone who does not let go until she is spent with exhaustion after the practice or match is over; someone who is willing to do all of these things every day with the same consistency of effort; someone whose passion for her teammates' success is bivouacked in her soul; someone who is a *servant leader* even though she may never have heard the phrase.

MAKE ROOM FOR THE BEACH

The possibility that women's beach volleyball could become a sanctioned NCAA sport is intriguing to me because the results of such a decision could impact indoor volleyball in ways we haven't imagined. Never underestimate the attraction of an environment where scantily clad coeds can be watched without the threat of arrest or restraining order. If you could add a ten-minute halftime show where fraternity lads blow up cats wearing the opponent's school colors, we might finally attract undergraduates to a non-revenue sport.

I believe that with the arrival of women's beach volleyball there is a good chance that the indoor six-person game might go the way of six-person women's basketball, meaning that there might be a few outposts in Nebraska, South Dakota, and areas of the country with a significant Amish population that would continue to play it, but it would be deader than keeping one foot on the floor on date night at the collegiate level.

Why? Beach volleyball has one significant advantage over the indoor game. The biggest challenge in indoor volleyball is that we have too many people on the court. In basketball there are five players and 5,000 square feet to cover. In volleyball there are six people and 900 square feet. A player can't take three steps without running into a teammate standing up in her base position. To create a level playing field, make Stanford, Hawaii, and Texas play with eight people on their side of the court. The defending national champion, should have to play with nine people and an alert umpire with an anal attention to overlaps. The difference between organizing two people and six people is the difference between two and six on a Richter scale.

Athletic directors and coaches might favor beach volleyball over indoor volleyball because they mistakenly believe their team would have the opportunity to be more nationally competitive in the two-woman game. Their thinking would go like this: We aren't able to recruit the explosive 6-foot-4-inch players that are required to advance to a Final Four; we have a better chance of landing those 5-foot-9-inch kids who are great ball handlers.

They would be wrong. How many truly great liberos have you seen in the past five years? Just because someone is less than 5-foot-9, plays volleyball, and is not explosive does not guarantee she can handle the ball any better than the kid bagging the ice cream on top of your bread at the local Piggly Wiggly. While junior volleyball has impacted technical skills, bracelet and T-shirt sales, and the pocketbooks of qualifier hosts, it has not done much to teach court awareness and a sense of the game. The few extraordinary ball handlers available are going to be recruited by the same schools that are getting commitments today from the kids blessed with vertical jumps and arm speed.

But hey, I'm for it. The Olympics made me an advocate for beach volleyball. I am awed by the commitment that Kerri Walsh and Misty May-Treanor made to become the dominant team in women's beach volleyball. What I admire most is not just their natural talent—blocking and attacking for Walsh, defense and pursuit for May—but their ability to better the ball no matter how difficult the first contact is. Other teams can make the first emergency play, but rarely do have the ability and tenacity to better the ball on the next contact like Misty and Kerri.

So I am for NCAA women's beach volleyball with the following caveats:

An event should consist of the best three of five matches. Matches are scored like the Olympics, two sets to twenty-one points with a third set to fifteen, if needed. Mid-majors and directional schools should be given the opportunity to wear uniforms with primary colors.

The coaches of each team choose which of their teams is going to play one through five, similar to the way the Ryder Cup is played.

The order is placed in a sealed envelope and given to the head referee. In other words, you do not have to play your best team in the No. 1 spot. This brings an element of gamesmanship and luck into play, something that will send the power conferences to the medicine cabinet, but will be a delight to fans and give opportunity for success to less talented teams.

Teams have to wear to the Ruben Acosta Signature line of beach volleyball apparel, keeping in mind that part of the attraction of this sport is the ambience (voyeurism) that beach culture has created. Culottes are not allowed.

Each university can choose the type of "sand" it plays on. The texture can vary from heavy river sand in the upper Midwest to pea gravel in southern Illinois to the ground microscopic snails of Hawaii's north shore. City universities can play on chipped asphalt and glass, and Ivy League schools on anything you can compost.

Fans admitted to a beach volleyball event would have their fingerprints scanned upon entry, making it easier to identify and locate the stalkers and sex offenders who are less likely to purchase season tickets to women's sports where the athletes are covered with armor, like fencing and lacrosse.

Finally, every host school is allowed to say over the public address system when the matches begin, "Welcome to the Beach!" even if the nearest ocean is the one where the ice is melting faster than a coach can signal for a sub after a shanked serve.

A DIFFERENT WAY TO LEAD

In 1981 I decided to run a side-out system where the attackers would call their sets instead of the setter. Prior to the serve each attacker would flash a hand signal indicating the location and tempo of the set. My primary purpose was to engage the attackers mentally in the process. Most of the time we ran the same three sets in a three-hitter system: a shoot set to the left side attacker, a front quick to the middle attacker, and a back set to the right-side attacker. These three sets were complemented with crosses, 31s, and back 2s. The slide was still a million daydreams away.

Late in the season we were playing a match against a conference opponent and in the final game, one of our outside hitters flashed four fingers, indicating a shoot set to the pin. The outside hitter was Julie Hermann, who later became the head volleyball coach at Tennessee and is now the senior women's administrator at Louisville. Julie has become one of the most talented and influential female athletic administrators in the country. In 2000 she chaired the Division 1 Volleyball Committee.

When Julie was a player, I liked to tell her that she was a slow but thorough learner, meaning that if she had fifteen years of eligibility she might become the best player in the country. At 6 feet, she was tall and physically strong but she had only two speeds—stop and go—and sometimes got them confused.

The setter was Mary Buysse, who later as Mary Byrne became the head volleyball coach at South Dakota State and North Carolina State. Mary was undersized, but made up for her lack of stature with competitiveness and courage. When we ran a 6-2 offense she would try to slip into the front row before I could make a substitution. She played with a chip on her shoulder that she leveraged into leadership. Her talent was winning.

At a critical point in the match Julie signaled for a 4-set and then proceeded to hit the set a boxcar wide of the left sideline. At the time, Julie Hermann was the antithesis of Mary Buysse. Julie was tall; Mary was short. Mary was analytical and Julie's modus operandi was surprise. Julie got to play all six rotations and Mary, despite being one of the top players in the league, was usually subbed out in the front row because of her blocking limitations.

I'm sure the injustice of all this played in Mary's mind as she watched Julie's attack bounce into the bleachers for an opponent point. Mary's countenance was that of an Australian sheepdog. She was constantly nipping at the heels of her teammates, keeping them organized, and she did it with the humor of a badger.

As our team returned to the serve-receive formation, Julie again signaled for a 4-set. Mary Buysse did not hesitate. She gave Julie a signal of her own, the universal middle digit, signifying not only that she wouldn't be seeing the ball on the next set but perhaps not for the rest of the match. Sometimes leadership can be both inelegant and precise.

RECRUITING AND MORELS

Coaching has to be one of the strangest professions. It has about as much potential for intimacy as being a gunfighter. The more responsibility you have, the less likely you are to share information with other coaches. Second assistants and graduate assistants love going to conventions and junior tournaments where they have the opportunity to talk with their peers about everything. Information is power. When you aren't making much money and don't have much control over what your responsibilities are, sharing a juicy tidbit about some new way your team is lifting weights or making a drop-step can be pretty heady stuff.

Head coaches lose sleep over things like this. I don't know how many times I've said to an assistant coach before she heads out the door to a junior tournament, "Remember, loose lips sink ships." Of course, because assistant coaches are too young to recognize a slogan that adorned World War II posters, I have to explain exactly what I mean.

"Don't talk about who we are recruiting, especially that hurdler from Chanute, Kansas that nobody else knows about. Don't tell anyone that we're working on a 6-2 offense in practice. Don't tell anyone that Smith had arthroscopic surgery. Don't tell them why I'm staying here in Lincoln, Nebraska, instead of going with you to Indianapolis to sit in a warehouse from 8 a.m. until 11 p.m. for three days watching sixty-four teams, each comprised of ten teenagers who will never play for Nebraska Volleyball, just so that the two players in the tournament we are interested in can look up and see that we are still interested."

I don't know any head coach who can look you in the eye without a beer in his hand and two or three in his gut and tell you anything but, "I hate recruiting." When you do meet someone who seems to enjoy it (as evidenced by the number of handwritten letters they produce daily or that you've never been to a junior tournament where they were not in the lobby having an apparently fascinating discussion on the nuances of rally score with a junior coach who is wearing flip-flops in January), you feel like throwing up.

What makes it really bad is that the results from recruiting can appear to be so arbitrary. We can all tell stories about the kid we worked hard to recruit only to lose her at the last second to the school she really wanted to attend when they decided that since their options were down to an outside hitter with one eye or a setter with bad hands, they might as well offer a scholarship to the girl we've already had the sports information director prepare a release on.

If we're lucky, we've had the opposite happen as well. Because we lost Heather to Penn State, Jenny to Stanford, Wendy to New Mexico, and Wendy's sister to a nunnery, we go ahead and offer a grant-in-aid to a local girl named Agatha who appears to have none of the genetics or technical skills we would normally recruit, noting that NCAA rules require us to emphasize that scholarships are a one-year commitment, only to have Agatha become an all-conference outside hitter and team captain her junior and senior seasons.

Her development and our insight into her special qualities allow her to live on in banquet speeches and the occasional motivational speech between the second and third games when we find ourselves down 0-2 because of a notable lack of effort, long after Agatha has graduated and gotten an MBA at an Ivy League institution that we never thought she would be admitted to.

Recruiting has about as much logic to it as looking for morel mushrooms in the spring. There are all kind of adages that supposedly tell you when, where, and under what conditions you are most likely to find the clusters of morels that sometimes appear in early May in Nebraska. "Look for them when the lilacs bloom." "Look for them under a dead elm tree." "Look for them under old fence lines." "Look for them on the north side of a riverbank." "Look for them when the ground temperature reaches 70 degrees." "Look for them after a spring shower."

There is some truth and a few mushrooms in all of these sayings. But if I had to say what I believe the truest thing about finding mushrooms is, it would be this: "You won't find any if you don't look, and when you do find them in a particular place, it only makes sense afterward."

This is true with recruiting as well. I can't always predict where a recruit is going to go, especially if we are recruiting her. But after she makes her decision and I've watched her develop and play at the college of her choice, it almost always makes sense. The truth is, most recruits choose the right place to go in the same way that in hindsight, mushrooms choose the right spot to appear.

How does this happen? When we recruit someone, we like to appeal to what we believe that person wants. We are goal-oriented. Sport is goal-oriented. One of the things that makes sport enjoyable is that there is a sense of finality to it. It can be measured. And so it seems only right that measurable things would be of interest to a recruit. We give them a litany of facts.

"Nebraska Volleyball has won twenty-eight conference championships and has played in ten Final Fours in the past twenty-one years. Nebraska Volleyball leads the nation in All-Americans and Academic All-Americans. We've spent over a million and a half dollars on our academic support center and we serve roast beef and tacos for dinner."

These facts may have some importance in attracting a recruit initially and allowing our school to be among the five she visits, but I think the actual decision making is based less on facts than on intuition; less on media guides than on sniffing. Recruits are like mushrooms. They have their own secret agenda for deciding where they are going to appear. Let me document my mushrooms.

At Nebraska we ended up signing a recruit who went on to earn multiple All-American honors and play on the U.S. Olympic team because, among other things, she loved competing in the color red. Another top recruit from a Southern state said her final decision came down to Nebraska because she wouldn't have to adjust to a new time zone.

We lost a top setter recruit because after watching a practice, she determined that Nebraska wasn't disciplined enough. This, despite the fact that Nebraska Volleyball had a reputation as one of the most disciplined women's intercollegiate programs in the country. When asked to explain what she meant by "discipline," she said, "the Nebraska players didn't tape their fingers and they seemed to be enjoying each other too much as they stretched before practice," an indication in her opinion of "a lack of intensity."

When you get this kind of response from a recruit, it doesn't do any good to argue or present your case in a logical manner. It wouldn't help to show a PowerPoint of "disciplined play" or call up former players who could testify as to the intensity of our practices, anymore than it would do any good to scream at the ground under a rotting elm tree, "Mushrooms, where the heck are you?"

Recruits sniff out a program the same way a retriever sniffs out the backyard. While you're talking about conference championships, they're circling around the notion that you may always have pens in your pocket. While you're talking about discipline and goal-setting, they're thinking about this cool place called "Buster's" they saw on the way in from the airport. While you're talking about the national ranking of the business college, which from your weekly telephone conversations is what the recruit's father thinks she eventually will major in, the recruit is wondering why Nebraska doesn't have ichthyology. While you're talking to the team captain about the conservative Christian upbringing of the prospective recruit, she is asking her team host if they are going to meet any football players.

So is there anything that can we learn from all of this? Yes, I think there is. First, it makes absolutely no sense to ever alter your behavior in any way because of who you think a recruit is. If you carry five pens in your pocket, so be it. If you listen to classical music in the car, don't buy alternative rock to play on the trip from the airport. If you don't have a major in marine biology, don't make a presentation on how ecology of the prairie would really prepare one for a graduate degree in marine biology because, after all, the prairie was once an ocean.

While you are making these changes to try to speak to what you think is the focus of your next outside hitter, she is feeling, not thinking. She is deciding whether she can trust you. And if, God forbid, she chooses your school because you don't dress like a hardware salesman or because you played songs from her favorite group on the way to practice or because you said you'd consider her as a primary passer when you'd rather pass with your golden retriever, then you've got a real problem. You're stuck for four years with someone who didn't get what she wanted, and you can bet that her volleyball instincts aren't any better than her ability to figure you out.

SNAKES, RECRUITS, AND SERENDIPITY

I have a friend who owns an ice cream shop in Northern Colorado who told me a story that would seem highly unlikely if it had not come from a conservative gentleman who is not given to exaggeration.

Several years ago he was driving on a gravel road near a local reservoir when he came around a bend and saw what appeared to be a log lying across the road. He was traveling too fast to stop, and to leave the road might cause even more injury, so he did the best he could to slow down before running over what turned out to be not a log, but an enormous snake.

He estimated the snake to be between 18 and 20 feet long with a diameter of more than a foot. It was a mottled green, yellow, and brown, had two large indentations where the four wheels of the car had run over it, and at first appeared to be dead. He wanted to put the snake into the boot of the car because he was convinced nobody would believe his story, but before he could figure out a way to lift a 300-pound snake, it took off for a nearby marsh at what he described as *incredible speed*, almost as fast as he ran to his car.

If you live long enough, you are going to see some strange things in your life. I saw a young black bear sitting in the parking lot of the public library last fall in the same week that the Rockies won the National League pennant and President Bush said that Americans might want to consider exploring energy options other than oil. When I arrived home from hearing the snake story, I Googled *large green* and *yellow constrictor* and came up with three options. The snake could be a python, a boa constrictor or an anaconda, most likely a former pet that reached a critical mass that allowed it to determine its own destiny or at least encourage its owner to set it free in a state wildlife refuge.

Before you discount the story, keep in mind that there are now alligators living in the Colorado River near Alamosa, a mountain lion was killed within the Omaha city limits, and a colony of tropical parrots has lived on the South Side of Chicago for decades. That doesn't even consider the possibilities in Florida where non-native plants, animals, and insects are creating a Jurassic Park in the Everglades.

When I was coaching I sometimes dreamed that a talented, skilled, unrecruited, non-native volleyball player would show up on campus during the summer and ask if she could try out for the volleyball team as she ducked under the 6-foot-5-inch threshold that led to my office. Perhaps she would be a foreign student whose father or mother was on sabbatical teaching anthropology or economics in an exchange program.

Something like this has actually happened at least once that I know of. In her second year as head coach of the University of Florida, Mary Wise was introduced to Aycan Gokberk by Aycan's uncle, a professor in the food and science department. Aycan, who was working as a nanny for her uncle's family in Gainesville, happened to be a 17-year-old member of the Turkish national volleyball team. Can you say "jackpot"?

From 1993 through 1995 Gokberk earned three All-American certificates and was one of the most dominant players in the country. She currently holds or shares over forty records for the Gators.

This story reminds me of that Visa commercial where a lady discovers a Van Gogh on the back of an Elvis painting she bought at a garage sale. I doubt if that commercial has prompted many of us to start investing in velvet paintings on the chance that we're going to fund our children's junior volleyball development by accumulating bad art.

I do believe there are a couple of things we can learn from the Aycan Gokberk story. One is that Coach Wise was very lucky. An American player of Gokberk's skill and athleticism would not slip through the radar of recruiting gurus and the Palm Pilots of assistant coaches today. Her name would regularly appear on chat lines and lips of volleyball foamers.

The second and more important observation is this: In my opinion, it is highly unlikely that a coach can build a *consistent* Top 25 program in any women's sport (including volleyball) without actively recruiting foreign athletes, and to not do so will seem in hindsight as provincial as recruiting only athletes born in Mississippi or volleyball players who are members of the Mennonite Church.

We owe it to American players to recruit outstanding foreign talent. Foreign athletes are frequently more experienced, more mature, more grateful, and sometimes come without the sense of entitlement that embellishes the families and graduates of junior volleyball programs.

Foreign athletes are the competition that our children are going to face the rest of their lives in industry, research, sales, technology, the arts and sciences. Because college graduates in every other country in the world already speak our language, they are at a tremendous competitive advantage. We need them at least as much as they need us. In time, the term "foreign" will seem as remote and archaic as pinnies and culottes.

I believe coaches have two options. You can wait and pray that you will be lucky and that one day walking into your office will be a potential ace attacker from Cuba assigned to program your computer. (About as likely as finding an anaconda crossing the highway in Larimer County, Colorado.) Or, you can do what Americans have always done best: saddle up and go get 'em.

DANCE CARD

Journal Entry: October 15, 1987

I made my first "home visit" to a 1987-88 volleyball recruit last night. Recruiting ranks somewhere between shoveling snow and pulling bindweed as my favorite thing to do. It's not that I don't enjoy meeting with families and talking about the University of Nebraska. On the contrary, I love sharing information about the tradition and opportunities available to someone playing volleyball at Nebraska. It's that I don't enjoy the feeling of vulnerability that comes from a 40-year-old man trying to persuade a 17-year-old girl to come to the dance.

What makes this process bearable is knowing that every hour spent on recruiting makes my job significantly more interesting down the road. The better students and athletes learn faster, require less energy to motivate, and continue to develop throughout their collegiate careers. And so I find myself bouncing along a country road in the foothills by the Missouri River trying to find a bridge that serves as a landmark in the directions the recruit has provided.

After searching for several minutes I pull into a farmhouse driveway and before I can ask directions, a man in bib overalls opens the screen door and asks me which school I'm from. Before I can answer he tells me: "Oklahoma was asking for directions last night, and Iowa the night before. As a matter of fact, hardly a night has gone by in the past two weeks that some volleyball coach didn't stop to ask how to get to the Kruse place." He seems to be taking great pleasure in his role as gatekeeper.

I feel like throwing up, but I remember the speech I gave to my players earlier in the day about remaining calm and strong under stress, and so I hold out my hand and say, "Hi, I'm Terry Pettit, the volleyball coach at the University of Nebraska, the school that Janet's going to play for next fall." Gulp.

It turns out the farmer is the father-in-law of one of my former players and he, like everyone else, feels confident Janet will go to Nebraska. The problem is that it's not "everyone else's" decision. And besides that, everyone is getting a kick at seeing all these coaches drive down this muddy road.

The visit goes well. Janet plans to make an official visit to Nebraska in late October. Even though she lives an hour and a half from the University I ask if she would like us to fly her in for her official visit, as we would do with a recruit from out of state. This makes no sense in terms of time or efficiency, but the last thing I want her to feel is that we are taking her for granted because she's from Nebraska. She considers my offer, considers my sanity, and then says, "No, it would be much easier just to drive in."

After two chocolate chip brownies, six handshakes, a visit to the garage to see the 4-week-old kittens, lengthy discussions on academic counseling, strength training, next year's schedule, the baggy shorts girl basketball players wear, and what last year's graduates are doing, I am on my way down the drive thinking about what a great player Janet will be; hoping she has a good visit in October; hoping her parents realize what a great opportunity she has; hoping she comes to the dance.

IN BREATHING AND CONSPIRING TOGETHER, THE GLORY

In the 1989 Academy Award-winning film *Glory,* Matthew Broderick plays Colonel Robert G. Shaw, a white officer in the Union Army who leads the 54th Massachusetts Volunteer Regiment, which, apart from the officers, was one of the first units of the U.S. Army to be comprised entirely of African-Americans.

In the penultimate scene in the movie, Colonel Shaw climbs down from his horse and joins his men as they walk along the beach toward battle and impending death. The act of dismounting and walking among his regiment is a metaphor that is at the heart of great leadership.

In the architecture of championship teams and organizations, leadership rarely arrives from long distance, either physically or emotionally. Whether it is a successful machine shop, a construction site, or an athletic department, the best leader is not in a remote tower or a corner office that requires a team member to run a gauntlet of passwords and advance appointments. In the best teams the head coach/CEO is on the floor interacting with machinists, coaches, finish carpenters, and point guards.

In unhealthy organizations the CEO discourages the dissemination of information. Team members are kept from sharing ideas with each other; e-mails move in only one direction. Ultimately, a climate of fear emerges that makes creative collaboration impossible, followed quickly by a malaise of mistrust that settles into the organization like a virus.

When there is a morale problem in a family, children and pets are the first to become aware that something isn't right. In a larger organization, like an athletic department, the canaries are the service personnel, the secretaries, and the custodians.

Why is this? Because coaches, assistant athletic directors, and middle managers may be so busy trying to establish their relationship with a CEO that they disregard the unhealthy symptoms that surround them. Concern for their power base, and in some cases their survival, coupled with a rising tide of fear, can allow them to ignore the unhealthy management practices that are causing them to lose sleep at night and scan the want ads of professional journals.

If you really want to know how a CEO's leadership is impacting a team or department, have lunch with the maintenance crew. Custodians and secretaries are not focused on whether they are about to be promoted, moved to an office with a view, or if their next company car is a Lexus, but they are quick to notice whether the CEO remembers their name, asks how their family is doing, maintains eye contact, and seems enthusiastic about their performance. Their focus is on whether the CEO is genuinely interested in their well being, and they can smell a leader who lacks authenticity quicker than their boss can ask for coffee.

Here are things to look for in evaluating your team's leadership:

Extraordinary leaders lead from the front of the people to whom they are providing leadership, particularly in difficult times. Trust is built when a leader stands before a community (or a team) even when he isn't sure what the next move is; even when he may question his own judgment; even when he is not sure the goal is reachable. To retreat during difficult times is to invite the jackals of rumor, innuendo, and false information.

On healthy teams, information doesn't move in just one direction or even two directions; information moves in thousands of ways as team members are encouraged to interact with suggestions, observations, celebrations, and intimacy. Creating a climate of trust is dependent upon intimacy and is at least as important as measurable goals in the journey of a championship team or department.

Extraordinary leaders surround themselves with people who have complementary talents and they give those people the opportunity, resources, and mentoring to become extraordinary leaders themselves. Unhealthy leaders allow their egos to become their compass. They believe the old lie that they are not only the smartest person in the room but smarter than the rest of the team members combined. They may ask for input, but it is basically a charade, and in the end they choose the colors of the wastebaskets in the restroom.

Great leaders may provide a great deal of direction when the team is in crisis or when a specific challenge matches their own talents, but for the most part, they are coaching, not pushing; they are moving toward collaboration at every opportunity. One of their major goals is to help develop as many leaders as possible throughout the organization. They can do this is by motivating team members with the observation that they already have the right stuff to be extraordinary. Team members may need to sharpen fundamentals or skills, they may need to leverage their talents, but they do not need to alter their DNA.

While it seems simple to say that a team reflects its leadership, it is also true. A leader models the culture he hopes to create. If he says he values integrity and collaboration but his actions are manipulative, secretive and abusive, the disconnection between what he says and how he acts can create a neurotic organization in which even the most talented and motivated team members may come to believe they are part of the problem. They either get out if they are fortunate enough, or they settle into the residue of anger and fear that is created by the CEO's lack of authenticity.

In contemporary life, the word conspiracy has taken on negative implications. Its original meaning was "we breathe together." What a beautiful description of collaborative teamwork. With extraordinary leadership, each team member feels he is in a leadership role. He believes that his talents and commitment are essential to the success of the team, and he has been encouraged to discover or create even better ways to meet the challenges before him.

In the final scene of *Glory,* Colonel Shaw continues to press forward even after two bullets have slowed him, until he is finally dropped by a third. His death causes his men to stand and charge Fort Wagner as they respond to his ultimate leadership.

While extraordinary leadership rarely requires such a dramatic decision, what we need right now is for the men and women in leadership roles to dismount and walk among their teammates. We need them to recruit and empower exceptional talent. We need to them to breathe together. We need a conspiracy of hope.

A FIELD GUIDE TO LEADERSHIP BEHAVIORS

Leadership, like coaching, is one of the most complex things that I know of. If we had a field guide to leadership it would contain thousands of decisions, some of them paradoxical and contradictory. Here are some I would include:

• Leadership is being collaborative with your assistant coaches and giving them the opportunity to take complete responsibility for a specific area of the program, then giving them the resources and mentoring to be successful.

• Leadership is wooing and educating an administrator who can make a difference in your program, and who becomes emotionally engaged in your program's development.

• Leadership is waiting for tomorrow's practice before you respond to a disappointing effort in tonight's match. Video, input from assistant coaches, and reflection on your own preparation and game coaching decisions will help you give a more focused response to your team.

• Leadership is hiring local and regional coaches to work your camps even when they may not have as much experience as people you could bring in from the outside. Leadership is developing the coaches in your geographical area.

• Leadership is working backward from a goal. First, we make the decision to reach a specific target. Then we recruit the talent we need to reach the target. Finally, we commit to the behaviors that give us the best opportunity to reach our goal.

• Leadership is modeling the behavior you would like to see from players when they are under stress.

• Leadership is asking yourself before you request a meeting with a player, "Am I doing this for her benefit or mine?" If it is the latter, you don't need to meet.

• Leadership is leveraging the strengths of your team and individual players rather than focusing on their weaknesses.

• Leadership is letting go of ego when responding to disappointing losses or remarkable wins.

• Leadership is recognizing the difference between talent and skill: what can't be taught and what can.

• Leadership is not just training fundamentals, but creating an environment where learning is more likely to take place.

• Leadership is changing behavior.

• Leadership understands the difference between focusing on style or fundamentals: between bouncing the ball three times before the serve and being balanced on the front foot at contact.

• When purpose and goals collide, leadership chooses purpose.

• Leadership moves from directing to coaching to collaboration.

• Leadership without self-disclosure cannot develop trust.

• Leadership chooses to put itself in uncomfortable situations and to train its team to embrace being uncomfortable as they develop.

• Leadership does not worship heroes, but trains and gives the opportunity for heroic behavior.

• Leadership listens to James Taylor on the radio and asks, "How does this song apply to my team?" Leadership goes to Wal-Mart and asks, "What does the clerk do better than me?" Leadership watches a football game and notices that a defensive back shadows the opponent's best receiver wherever he goes. Leadership asks, "What is the application to the libero?" Leadership asks, "How do they train the turn at the end of the pool?" Leadership adapts. Leadership innovates. Leadership creates its own university where everything it experiences may have application to how a 17-year-old moves to the ball.

• Leadership tells stories. There was girl who tried out as a walk-on for the volleyball team. She came from an area of the state where there are blue highways and no four-lane roads, where pelicans migrate to small sand hill ponds in the summer. The men wear hats or farm implement caps when driving, and they come into town for coffee.

She was pretty and had fast-twitch muscles, but her stature and the length of her arms meant she would have difficulty blocking. She was a good student and had an even better countenance. On a team of fourteen, she would never rise above eleven.

She was on the team for three years. A good practice player who rarely entered a game, she impacted the team G.P.A. more than matches. Once, when entering the coach's office after her first year and asking what she could do to get better, an inexperienced head coach told her, "You have a better chance of flying across the street to the gymnasium than contributing to this team." She laughed and went home, resolved to accomplish all the things the coach had questioned.

It would be nice if this story had a dramatic ending. Something like the player entering a match with the home team down in the fifth game of a regional championship, and she would go back beneath the balcony and unleash a string of unpassable serves

85

that would send the opponent spinning into a time-out before the inevitable defeat. A rainbow of serves that meant that every minute of shagging balls, lifting weights, carrying equipment, playing roles, and wearing the numbers of opponents was worthwhile because of this special moment.

But that never happened. She never entered the game at a critical moment. She never had the opportunity to serve for the regional championship. Her shining moments came in practice when the "B" team plus an assistant coach would beat the first team in a wash drill. Sometimes the first assistant would pull her aside and whisper, "Great job today in practice."

She graduated and earned a master's degree in physical therapy. She married and had a daughter. Divorced. She was a success in business and continued to reinvent herself with bodybuilding first, then religion, then leadership and management. She learned to play poker and to empower her employees. At every turn she kept in touch with her coach and her team. In this respect, she was like an upland retriever that forges into the wood to hunt but every now and then returns to make eye contact, to make sure you are still there.

What she may not know is how important these contacts were to the coach as well. (Does the dog greeting us at the door know that we would wag if we could?)

So what does this mean? Something happened that was good. Despite the head coach's inexperience, despite the absence of a dramatic moment in a career spent on the "B" side of the net, she may have sensed that he cared about her development, or maybe we should allow for one of the most important ingredients in leadership, that for which we have no word other than grace.

THE ART OF VOLLEYBALL

I like to imagine what Sun Tzu, the heroic Chinese general and author of *The Art of War,* would have written if his passion had been coaching volleyball instead of military strategy. It might have gone like this:

I. There are three ways to disarm the opponent with the serve:
1. Serve to the receiver whose eyes refuse to meet yours.
2. Serve to the receiver who has one arm longer than the other.
3. Serve to the receiver who looks for her mother to fill her water bottle.

II. Try to disrupt cooperation between the opponent's setter and her quick attacker with one of the following tactics:
1. Have your team captain engage the opposing setter with an interesting story.
2. Have your blockers wear Roman numerals.
3. Squint and pretend there is no danger.

III. If the opponent's players march into the arena angrily and remain facing your team for a long time without serving or retreating, the situation demands a time-out with loud incomprehensible music.

IV. When the stress of the season starts to impact your mental health, realize this truth: the head coaches of Olympic sports are not fired until football has a winning season.

V. When the opponent sends out only small defensive players to hit in the warm-up, beware: it is a trick or you have scheduled a soccer team by mistake.

VI. If the campus you are visiting should harbor hilly country, large cardboard boxes, and hollow garbage cans filled with excessive paper, beware: the opponent has received a shipment from Nike.

VII. There are three dangerous flaws that may affect a coach and his team:
1. A lack of arm speed, which leads to an indifferent assault.
2. A senior who has fallen in love for the first time, which leads to aimless play.
3. Signaling on the wrong side of the clipboard, which leads to confusion for the server and great delight for the fans.

VIII. Fear the opponent who arrives by charter jet. Be suspicious of the opponent who arrives by motor coach. Schedule frequently the opponent who arrives in a Dodge Caravan.

IX. If over-matched with the opponent, do not invite the athletic director to watch your ineptitude.

X. In the recruiting process, beware the junior coach who has the logos of Final Four participants stitched to his warm-up.

XI. If the opposing setter tapes her fingers, she has spent countless hours in training. If the opposing coach tapes his fingers, he has spent countless hours in therapy.

XII. Regard your players as your children and they will follow you into the darkest valleys. Ask them to set aside their cell phones and they will consider you a stranger.

XIII. All volleyball is based on deception.
1. The setter hopes to deceive the middle blocker by moving her hips.
2. The outside hitter hopes to deceive the digger with a tip and an aggressive approach.
3. The coach hopes to deceive the fans by scheduling ghosts in the preconference season.

XIV. When the foolish assistant mistakes generosity for vulnerability in the countenance of the head coach, the assistant has begun the long, painful journey to another camp.

XV. When the head coach begins to believe that the system is the key to his success and stops recruiting great talent, he is on a path to becoming a barista.

XVI. When dust is rising on the horizon, it is a sign that the enemy is approaching or perhaps that we have once again been assigned to a building that revenue sports have abandoned.

XVII. When the opposing coach greets you with the phrase, "Welcome to the enchanted valley," brace yourself from showing enthusiasm at the opportunity to wage a battle with the entitled.

XVIII. When calling a time-out consider the following:
1. Do not ask a rhetorical question.
2. Ignore the player searching for her boyfriend in the stands.
3. Do not identify the person that you do not intend to serve.

XIX. Experience is only valuable with reflection. A wise coach begins every evaluation with the phrase, "How did we do this to ourselves?"

COACHING AND PARENTING

I have a friend who tells me that in 1953 he could fix about anything on a Chevy with a screwdriver and crescent wrench. Those days are gone. So, too, are the days when "organized sport" meant the kids in the neighborhood gathering at the end of the block, without adults, to negotiate who would play on which team, who would be chosen last, and who would play right field.

Some people argue that in moving from a culture of spontaneous play to a culture of organized sport, we have improved our kids' technical skills while neglecting the development of other skills, such as negotiation, initiative, communication, and the ability to solve problems without adult intervention. To put it bluntly, we are over-organizing our kids' play and delaying their ability to develop skills that will help them the most as adults.

The more our culture relies on organized sport to teach our children how to play and compete, the more expectations parents have for the coaches who work with our kids. We want the coach to teach our kid how to play. We want our kid to play shortstop when she's not pitching. If our kid gets really good, we want her to be on an elite team so she can travel and develop at a faster pace. And, most importantly, we want the coach to make the experience painless. We do not want our children to suffer the indignity of being a substitute, a role player, or approach any scenario that might be interpreted as failure. We want all this for our children despite that success in our adult lives is mostly about dealing with bad hops, missed promotions, delayed gratification, and the occasional bounce of good luck.

This is a lot to ask of someone who has been trained as a history teacher, pipe fitter, or surgeon, or someone who is volunteering to coach because nobody else would. It is a lot to ask of a professional coach with a master's degree in sports psychology. Given that most of the people who coach our kids are not trained in coaching, it might be helpful to identify some characteristics of great coaching that are available to everyone regardless of experience. Here are some behaviors you might bring forth if you are asked to coach a team, and you might look for these same qualities in evaluating someone as a potential coach for your son or daughter. These characteristics are just as important if you're coaching the Little Chiefs or a college basketball team.

1. All great coaching begins with hope. Great coaching is communicating through posture, language, chalk talks, and intimate conversations the ultimate belief that good things are going to happen.

2. Great coaching is being able to communicate to an athlete that she already has the "right stuff" to get the job done. We may need to improve her fundamentals. We may need to work harder. We may need to make some adjustments, but we don't need a genetic transplant. We already have the DNA that, combined with hard work, will allow us to be great.

3. Great coaching is more concerned with the process and (parents take note) less concerned with the outcome. Are we committed to behaviors that lay the foundation for success? Are we on time? Do we look each other in the eye when we speak? Do we give great effort? Do we maintain the sacredness of the group by not voicing our frustrations outside the team? Do we encourage our teammates even when we are on the sidelines? Are we passionate in our commitment? Committing to new behaviors is as important to a team's success as a solid foundation is to a new house. It's quiet and it doesn't get much press, but nothing else can move forward without it.

4. Great coaching understands the need for risk and the value of failure. There is no growth without pain. The surest way to not win a championship is to try to protect your success. If you are in the presence of great coaching, the coach will ask you to become more uncomfortable than you want to be as you risk new roles, new techniques, and new expectations.

5. Great coaching understands that performance, whether individual or team, is based on trust. Athletes have the best chance for performing well when they trust themselves. Teams have the best chance for success when coaches and parents create a climate in which athletes believe that the adults' support for them is not based on their most recent performance. The support is unconditional. Athletes have the best chance to learn what trust is when they see it modeled by their parents and coaches.

The days of '53 Chevys and pick-up games are gone, and they are not likely to return unless our culture begins to place more value on neighborhood play and less dependency on minivans and over-organized sport. In the meantime, my wish is that everyone's son or daughter has the opportunity to play for a coach who is hopeful about the team's future, who believes your kid has the right stuff to get the job done, who encourages your son or daughter to commit to behaviors that will provide the best chance for success, and who creates an environment where kids have the opportunity to risk, rise, fall, and risk again.

Then again, these characteristics would make for great parenting as well.

TIME-OUT

When the time-out comes, what should I say?
If the play has been good, nothing is best:
  Perhaps a few clicks of the tongue,
A man urging a horse toward home;
"Giddy up" or "Whoa" the messages I send
While the manager is spilling water on the court,
And the second referee, an actuary
Who wouldn't know the difference
From a Buick and an overlap,
Tugs at our huddle with a reminder
To come back to where our opponent waits,
Organized, revitalized, and unfortunately without
Number 14 who has launched
Three consecutive passes into orbit.
And if the play is bad,
Should I say, "This display
Does not remind me of
Jazz, or ballet, or anything
Spontaneous and beautiful?"
Should I pull aside the team captain,
The one with the footwork and arm swing
Of a star fighter, and confide:
"Neither you nor I deserve this fate?"
Ah, conspire, *we breathe together.*
We join hands, the water bottles
Fall into the lap
Of the overweight trainer,
As I review the scales of modern volleyball:
"Move to the ball, Delay, Watch the dump!"
We bark allegiance to our school,
To each other, to the game.
We break.

WHAT I MISS MOST ABOUT COACHING

Not a day goes by since I left Nebraska Volleyball that someone doesn't ask me, "Do you miss it?" I could respond with a blank look and say, "Miss what?" But that would be unfair because even though I am asked the question all the time, it is fresh to them. My usual reply is, "Of course there are aspects of coaching that I really miss, but what pleases me most is that I get tremendous pleasure and satisfaction from watching a great coach (John Cook) and his talented team continue to have great success building a tradition of opportunity and excellence."

This response, while sounding a bit like a paragraph from the "Media Guide for Old Coaches" is helpful in several ways. First of all, it's true. I do have great appreciation that something I put so much of my life into continues to do well. What people are really saying is, "Are you doing OK? We appreciate what you did. We appreciate how we felt when we became so engaged in the competition that we became part of the event."

Yes, there are plenty of things that I miss. I miss watching a player have a breakthrough in her understanding of the game, when she makes the right decision at the right time, for the first time. I miss watching the players come on to the court, shy and alert as zebras before they begin to share the intimate bits of their day with each other that coaches aren't privy to, a network of communication and emotion that becomes the secret life of teams.

I miss watching videotape over and over until a pattern of vulnerability begins to emerge. No. 12 on Missouri doesn't move as well to her left as to her right on a line-to-line serve. The Kansas State setter always goes back to a hitter if she makes an unforced error early in a game, but late in a game she'll set someone else. If Florida loses two consecutive points in the first rotation they shift their reception pattern and set the outside hitter who is normally their third option.

It's like unraveling fishing line when you are standing in the middle of a spring creek and just around the bend rainbows are rising to caddis flies. The man who taught me to fly-fish once told me, "If you want to get serious about this (fly-fishing), you've got to love to untangle knots. Not just be willing to untangle knots. You've got to develop a love for knots." I love and miss searching for patterns that reveal strengths and weaknesses in an opponent.

I miss going for early morning walks on the day of a competition on a road trip in a new city. I miss staying up at night with the assistant coaches wondering whether the team realizes how difficult the next match will be. I miss looking into the countenance of the players before the match and seeing their noses flared for competition, their eyes looking past the game plan outlined on the whiteboard to a place farther back where their focus and commitment are moving toward trust.

I miss sitting in the locker room alone after the team has gone up to the Coliseum arena. I do not smoke, but I imagine the relaxation and anticipation that I feel sitting there by myself while the team is warming up above me is almost narcotic. We are prepared. We are ready. We are at home. Does it get any better than this? Not, at least, until the next time.

I miss walking out the door of the locker room, moving up the stairs in a predictably unpredictable pattern, moving among and with the fans, hearing words of encouragement floating through the air like maple seeds. I miss coming out from behind the curtain and the Nebraska bench, past the security guards and the paramedics, and it is all there. The band is playing. The opponent is energized by the fact that they will be playing against the best team in front of the largest crowd they will see all year. The visiting coach is keeping time to the band with his left foot. His assistant coach, dressed in a sweat suit in the school colors, is warming up the team with more purpose than ever. The general admission section has been full for an hour. The season ticket holders are greeting each other with the familiarity of the fans of a rock group who have traveled to every concert on this year's tour. The building is alive. This is a big match. This is a match we could possibly lose. The fans can hardly believe that they are this close to the court. They feel like they are part of the game. The players meet to join hands and recite their litany of love and responsibility one more time. No one can contain his enthusiasm. It is like dancing and watching yourself dance at the same time.

The whistle blows. We get to do it again.

COACHING REDUX

When I turned 61 years old last year, I thought that I had a few options. I could buy a Toyota Avalon, wear a black Kangol cap, and drive under the speed limit while making right turns for the rest of my life. Other options included fly-fishing, golf, and reading adventure magazines for free while nursing a decaf mocha at Barnes & Noble. For some reason, given these choices, I decided to become a volunteer coach for a junior volleyball team. What was I thinking?

It's not as if I'm unaware of the land mines in junior volleyball. After all, I spent a small chunk of my professional life in convention centers evaluating, eliminating, and praying that two or three talented junior players could be wooed to a university without a window on the ocean.

I also am aware of the potentially combustible combination of parents who feel more and more entitled with each dollar they spend on their collegiate volleyball investment plan, their daughter's indifference to non-negotiable behaviors, and the expectations of junior coaches who sometimes confuse knee socks with fundamentals.

I've always had a love-hate relationship with junior volleyball. On the one hand, my job as a head coach at the University of Nebraska would not have been possible without junior volleyball and the sacrifices junior coaches make to develop players so that when those players arrive at a university campus they know the difference between a drop step and doughnut.

On the other hand is my aversion to the accoutrements of what junior volleyball has become. There are 12-and-under teams that have more uniforms than the Lakers. There are clubs that have three coaches with laptops on the bench who must be recording something like, *"Jenny just got aced. Again."* There are clubs that make hundreds of thousands of dollars by overcharging other clubs for entry fees, taking kickbacks on food and hotel rooms, and whose greed makes Wall Street look like Greenpeace.

Some clubs post dollar signs on their Web sites with their coaches serving as agents for their best players, even at times encouraging a player to leave her initial college when it is determined that Olivia can play at a higher level. Some clubs discourage local colleges from recruiting their best players, but initiate phone calls and encourage these same local college coaches to take a look at players on the "B" and "C" squads. They are not interested in *fit* but rather which university will look best on the club Web site.

Other programs profess to mentor leadership skills, but leadership turns out to be a type of autocratic control that focuses on arbitrary rules concerning the color of hair ribbons, the length of knee socks, and the absence of parental interaction during tournaments.

And then there are statistics that show we have a higher percentage of girls participating in organized junior club programs (in all sports) at age 12 and under than ever before, yet the percentage of those still playing organized sport when they are 17 continues to decline. When you've been given monogrammed sweats, gym and travel bags, and you've flown across the country to play other teams decked out in professional gear when you're 12, you've pretty much hit the peak.

A couple of years ago I was the only parent of a daughter on a 12-and-under team who voted not to go to nationals if we qualified, partly because, among other things, we could not beat a team of rug rats six miles down the road. Why not just create a local World Series with a picnic? We could save thousands of dollars in travel while dodging convention center cough and runs to the bathroom from too much Jamba Juice.

So why, given my ambivalence about junior volleyball, did I choose to become a volunteer coach for a 14-and-under team? Because my daughter asked me. Actually, the conversation began three years ago when she said, "Dad, do you know anybody who could help me become a setter?" She knows I was a coach in a former lifetime, but it is no more real to her than imagining life without text messages.

It would be an understatement to say that my return to coaching was difficult. I was a volunteer assistant coach to a young head coach who valued my experience about as much as if I had a background in tuning oboes. I was not allowed on the bench because it made her uncomfortable, and when I suggested that we might consider teaching run-throughs in a posture less upright than a marching band, she would look at her watch. The only thing that would have made my return to coaching more awkward would be if I tried doing it wearing mukluks while lashed to a dogsled.

I came close to quitting twice, and I eventually did leave during the last month when I thought my frustration with the situation was not helpful to the team. I felt bad because I remembered all the club and high school coaches in Nebraska who must have overcome their own frustrations and how I benefited from their commitment. I would have left sooner, but my wife and daughter asked me to remember who I was doing this for, and so for twelve weeks I put on my six-year-old pair of Adidas, (my last perk from Nebraska) and headed out with my daughter to practice where I was given twenty minutes to run one drill any way I saw fit.

But here's the thing. In the middle of that drill, a girl from Eaton, Colorado, got into extension for the first time in her life, contacted the ball at the peak of her jump, snapped her wrist, and the ball hopped over the net like a rabbit with a purpose. I could not contain myself as I shouted "YES!" with the same enthusiasm and joy that I first did thirty-five years ago.

ME AND PAUL AND SPOONS ON THE TABLE

I have a friend named Paul who is a student of contemporary culture and who recently retired from coaching at a small private college east of the Elkhorn River. He had a good deal of success both as a teacher and a coach, and as he looks back on his career he's comfortable with what he sees. There are, however, a few things that concern him about the coaching profession.

He's concerned about the lack of grace, integrity, and intimacy that he sees among some of the *best* coaches in the volleyball community. He is an astute observer and on more than one occasion during my career he suggested a better option to a decision that I was considering. Frequently I took his advice and I thought you might be interested in some of his insights. (The quotes are Paul's. I placed my own observations in italics.)

"Coach P., there is an episode of "The Simpsons" where Homer is enlisted to prepare school lunches for Bart and Lisa. Homer fills Bart's lunch box with Grandpa's medications and places a drawing of lunch in Lisa's backpack. It's a funny scene because given Homer's level of competency and his value system that celebrates expediency, his decision strikes us as predictable. Homer never *chooses* to do the right thing. If he happens to make the right choice, it is by accident."

Paul says this as he is holding a can of Grain Belt Premium in his left hand and moving six spoons into a reception pattern on the kitchen table.

"It is not just the *result* of a coach's decision that we use to evaluate his career in the end, but his motivation, his character, and the values that inform his judgment. Decisions are the essence of leadership."

Paul then shared with me a litany of questionable decisions that have been made by volleyball coaches in the past few years while the spoons lay in a stack-left formation.

"I know a head coach who won a national championship and then informed one of his top recruits shortly before signing date that she would have to *gray-shirt* and enroll in a junior college if she wanted to be a part of the program, something that she was not informed of in the recruiting process. Either the coach couldn't count to twelve or decided to create some cap room for a transfer that suddenly become available."

I am not familiar with the term "gray-shirt" although that was the color of the jersey I wore in basketball practice as a member of the "C" team in high school. We called ourselves the "Go-Go Grays."

Paul continues, "There are the two prominent coaches in a BCS conference that were accused by their peers of knowingly recruiting athletes who had been paid to play professionally in Europe, a violation of NCAA rules. The coaches responded with a challenge that was more appropriate to "The Sopranos" than higher education when they said, 'Prove it.' "

My own experience with foreign players is somewhat mixed. We were able to recruit an exceptional defensive player from Sweden who played on a national championship team, and a middle blocker from Australia who turned out to be a defensive specialist. We later discovered that on the videotape we used to evaluate her, she was playing on a 6-foot net. We probably should have noticed the unlikely scenario of two 7-foot officials.

Paul then says, "I read about a head coach of a program that won a dozen consecutive conference championships and then lost a conference match for the first time in several years. Rather than graciously complimenting the opposing coach on a remarkable effort, the coach accused the opposing coach of deliberately throwing an earlier match to obtain a competitive advantage in the return match."

I doubt that this allegation is true because, with the exception of Paul, it is rare for any coach to acknowledge the tactical superiority of an opposing coach. I only coached against Paul's teams twice and both times he was very quick to commend our players, even when we were lucky to win a match due to an overzealous referee, poor lighting, and an inadvertent overlap that only someone with a background in code breaking could have uncovered.

"Then there was the head coach of a team that won the Division 1 national championship who refused to shake the extended hand of the opposing coach, and told him to **** off. The winning coach later said he was upset because the losing coach wanted to interact with him before the match and he didn't want to lose his focus."

I had heard this story from the losing coach three years earlier, and continue to be stunned by it. I usually saved my worst behavior for the locker room after the match.

Paul then shared his belief that there is a cadre of collegiate coaches who have worked to create a culture that maintains there is only *one way* to coach. "They believe there is only *one way to block, one way* to train your setter, *one way* to design a base defense. And what's even worse, that way is a secret and you have to promise that you will not share if it you are judged worthy enough to receive the information. It is an attitude more appropriate for the queue in a junior high cafeteria."

I'm not sure there is only one way to do anything. Several years ago some wag in California flew over the San Bernardino Mountains in a lawn chair with a pellet gun and 45 weather balloons. I would give him an A for ingenuity and an F for judgment. There were rumors the pilot (and I use the term loosely) was a high school volleyball coach who couldn't get his kids to communicate.

"How about this one," he says. "An assistant coach to one of our most experienced and successful head coaches decides that the head coach's inclusiveness is a weakness, and sees it as an opportunity to leverage his own career by trying to manipulate the head coach into retirement. Fortunately, the assistant coach is eventually confronted for what he is and sent packing."

There are only a few stories since the beginning of time. Unfortunately, one of them is an apprentice misinterpreting trust and opportunity for weakness. Paul told me there is an episode of "The Simpson's that deals with this theme. Krusty the Clown plays the part of an assistant coach who tries unsuccessfully to overthrow a volunteer head soccer coach named Ned Flanders.

"In the midst of all this bad behavior, is it really surprising when two student athletes at the encouragement of their parents decide to leave a program where the head coach is widely respected, not only for her success but her character? Their rationale boils down to this: They choose to not be integral members of a team that was poised to challenge for national prominence because their individual success had put them in a position to choose a program that has already won a national championship." Paul leaves the table to get another Grain Belt from the fridge and continues, "If sport prepares us for life, then the parents of these players are preparing their kids for a life where their children better not ever have to work through anything more difficult than a "Little Debbie."

I'm impressed with Paul's passion and I agree with him on this one. I tried to head off this scenario by painting the bleakest, most realistic picture that I could to parents about the plan I had for their daughter. It probably cost me a couple of recruits, but many parents were quite surprised and relieved when their daughters grew up and graduated without losing any fingers in the process.

When I asked Paul if there is a consistent theme in all of these scenarios, he replied, "These decisions were made by talented people who chose fear for a compass. Fear of losing a conference championship, fear of not winning a national championship, fear of not meeting expectations, fear that there might be something slightly better around the next curve, fear that if they do not win every game they are no longer relevant, fear that acknowledging that someone else is doing good things somehow takes away from their achievements. None of the scenarios involved coaches (or players) who were on the precipice of losing their jobs or scholarships."

He continued, "If a coach refuses to be intimate with his peers and does not recognize their achievements, he is missing out on one of the most rewarding benefits of coaching: a community of respect and trust." He then offered this final proclamation while lifting the last of his second and not penultimate Grain Belt, "Now is the time for our best coaches to replace fear with trust—trust that our peers' success does not diminish us; trust that we are relevant even when we do not win championships; trust that we do not need more trophies to validate our sense of purpose. We need to make decisions with the same compass that we would want someone else to use if we entrusted him to coach our son or daughter. We need to appreciate the talent, commitment, and effort of our peers who, after all, are the only ones who truly understand what a difficult challenge this profession is."

Paul is a better man than I am. But here's the good thing: I am a better man when I am lucky enough to be seated at the kitchen table with him, spoons spread out in formation, trying to decide how would we would deal with a jump server attacking the right hip of a passer in zone 1, both of us happy to have been a part of the game, both of us with a genuine love for the coaches who try to get better.

THE FINAL PHASE IN A COACHING LIFE

I once wrote a short story with the premise that because sound is based on vibration, everything we say continues to reverberate even as those vibrations become fainter and fainter. Some day in the not-too-distant future, we may have the technological means to recover every human interaction. I thought about this again last summer when our family was traveling through the Snowy Range about an hour and a half from our home in Northern Colorado.

To get there we take Highway 287, a two-lane road that travels north by northwest to Laramie, Wyoming, through rock formations, sage, and a high mesa. Route 287 is a dangerous road, particularly at night, when eighteen-wheelers traveling at high speeds, frequently intersecting country roads ("frogs" to the locals), relentless wind, and alcohol can create a lethal combination.

When we reach Laramie we take Highway 130 west to Centennial, a town that claims to have a population of 100 ranchers, dropouts, and characters. A placemat at the Bear Tree Café notes that the local attractions include, "Flat Top Mountain, the wind, and hippies." If there are rumors that Jerry Garcia still lives, they would place him in Centennial, Wyoming.

There is a ranch near Centennial that lies in one of the most beautiful valleys I have ever seen. It flanks the Little Laramie River, and one morning while crossing a meadow to the stream with a friend, we saw a herd of several hundred elk, as well as mule deer, whitetails, and later, moose tracks in the alders.

It is this type of setting that serves as an entrance to the Snowy Range and Medicine Bow Peak, an off-white monolith of quartzite that appears from a distance to be covered in snow. It is quite simply breathtaking, particularly if you view it from the alpine lake that sits below.

Rising 12,013 feet above sea level, Medicine Bow Peak is two billion years old, and the mountains beneath it are even older. Two-thirds of the way up the peak are the remains of a DC-4 aircraft, United Flight 409, which crashed in 1955, killing all sixty-six people on board. It is possible to climb up to the crash site and even up to the top of the peak where you can see back across the valley to Laramie, Highway 287, and on to Colorado and the beginning of the Great Plains.

It was in December 1993 that Mike English, the head women's volleyball coach at the University of Wyoming and an assistant coach were traveling on Highway 287, taking a shortcut to Denver where they were to board a flight on a journey to the Final Four in Madison, Wisconsin.

Mike had built a highly competitive volleyball program at Wyoming, one that defeated Stanford to advance to the final eight in 1989, and prior to his tenure in Laramie he developed a Top 20 program at the University of Missouri that challenged for Big 8 titles.

We had occasionally roomed together on the road when recruiting. Mike's development of the program at Missouri had a direct impact on the program I was building at Nebraska. We could compete against each other, make sarcastic remarks in passing while turning in our lineups, enjoy each others successes, and support each other when we faced the inevitable challenges that coaching brings. He was as popular with his peers as with his players and I, like almost everyone else in the volleyball community, considered him a good friend.

I think our friendship was based primarily on Mike's countenance. I don't think he had a manipulative bone in his body, and while he was extremely competitive, I think he had advanced to a place in his coaching where his focus was not on personal success but more about helping the people around him become successful.

That is the final and most important stage in a coach's development. It is when a coach has enough confidence to let go of fear as a primary motivation and begin to give back. The coach begins to see rival coaches as peers and not as adversaries. He is not threatened by the success of other coaches and programs. Laughter and self-acceptance begin to replace anxiety and innuendo. Mike had entered this stage, and it is one of the reasons people were so comfortable in his presence.

Like everyone else, I was overwhelmed when I learned of the accident. The information was scant and it wasn't until later that we learned the extent of Mike's injuries. The collision had been unavoidable when a pickup truck pulled off a country road into the path of the two coaches traveling in the dark toward the Final Four.

Mike spent the next seven years confined to a wheelchair. He never coached again. He sustained significant brain damage from the accident as well as other complications that led to his death in 2000. I still ache when I think about him and how much I miss his friendship.

But there are good thoughts, too. From the top of Medicine Bow Peak I like to imagine that you can see far, to the rim of the prairie, across Colorado, Nebraska, Kansas, and Missouri and on to the South and East, where his former assistant coaches and players are still feeling the ripples of his generosity and presence. In the gymnasiums where they coach, young players bark at the ball, take risks, and play with joy, knowing only that they are learning from someone who cares about them. They are loved and they don't know why.

A LETTER FROM A FRIEND

I first read "A Letter From a Friend" at the American Volleyball Coaches Association convention at the 2000 National Championship in Richmond, Virginia. The presentation was well received, but the interaction I had with the audience afterward was different depending upon the gender of the coach. Male coaches wanted to know who the speaker was in the letter. Female coaches usually said something like, "You write very well."

Dear Terry,

I've been meaning to get in touch with you for some time, but you know how things go during the season. It's amazing the cat gets fed and we don't set the kids out by the curb on trash days. I was hoping to see you in Richmond but I'm not going to make it, so this will have to do.

Sara has gone off to a small Christian college where she plans to be a vegetarian and not go to sporting events, so that leaves just the three of us at home. Ben is going into fourth grade, and he brought home a permission slip to join either the track club or the chess club. When I asked him which activity he wanted to take part in, my heart sank a little when he said the chess club. But I suppose chess is better than watching those Japanese cartoons where two-dimensional rodents try to speak without lips, so we spent about a week with me trying to teach him about the different pieces.

Each night we would work with a different movement. The pawns, king, queen, and the rook were pretty straightforward. He didn't even have too much trouble with the bishops. They're kind of like a guy who looks at you out of the corner of his eye—sneaky but in a predictable way. I thought he might have some trouble with the knight because let's face it, how can you explain why a knight moves the way it does? As Ben said, "It always ends up where it wasn't going." But the knight became Ben's favorite piece because, as he said to me once while taking a pawn and putting me in check at the same time, "The knight is the only piece that can move among and through its own men."

I thought the concepts of "check" and "checkmate" would be even harder for Ben. But one day after a volleyball game in which one of our attackers thought she heard a whistle on game point, froze, and caught the ball, it was Ben who reasoned after the game that "she probably thought she was in checkmate and whatever she did it probably wasn't going to work out."

I felt like I was in check myself for most of the year. Like you, I've been doing this for a long time now, but unlike you, the support here has been pretty uneven. On the same day this past summer that I found out we'd have to bus eight hours to the conference tournament, I ran into two of our assistant women's basketball coaches who were debating whether the money they had just spent on a machine that would write letters in long hand to several hundred recruits would help them as much as the new alligator attachés the head coach had purchased for the staff.

It's not that these are bad people, it's just that with so much money they have to think up ways to spend it. I'm not sure our senior women's administrator agrees with how much money is budgeted for women's basketball, but basically she's been neutered. Nobody reports to her any more. She prepares reports on graduation rates and compiles a directory of alumni. I'm not sure there is a piece in a chess game that describes what her role is. Maybe if the queen couldn't move, that would best describe her role.

But my biggest challenge this year wasn't the athletic department's indifference to Olympic sports or the lack of people willing to witness for women's volleyball at the NCAA level. My biggest challenge was who was going to play right-side hitter. We had very good players at every other position. Our H2's not flashy, but she's dependable. She can pass and she's got a look-away serve that could surprise a bishop. These are not Division 1 All-Americans. They are not the kids who were recruited by any of the "big boys," but they're good kids who through hard work and a little luck have developed into pretty good players.

I have been building this group for three years. And even when they were freshmen I sensed there was something special about them, not because they were skilled or highly recruited (they weren't). It was more because they listened. They wanted to be better. The H1 wrote me the summer before she arrived and asked for videotapes of a graduating senior that she admired so she could watch them and understand her role.

The middle blocker is a great athlete who turned down scholarships in basketball, soccer, and track (sports that she was better at in high school) because she liked the spontaneity of volleyball. She liked the fact that we didn't have to wear baggy shorts, there weren't too many time-outs, and everybody got to touch the ball.

My problems were with my right-side player. Carrie is a walk-on that Loretta had seen playing in the state basketball tournament while I was on a road trip three years ago. She's only 5-foot-8-inches, but very athletic, and she has an explosive jump.

It took her a year just to acclimate to a larger town. She came from a ranch out in the Panhandle and while the kids out there learn a certain kind of independence from branding calves and working through blizzards, it doesn't give them much opportunity to play junior ball and develop a sense of the game.

But that wasn't her biggest challenge. She earned a scholarship after her first year and I thought she might really take off, but she didn't. It was almost as though she had reached her goal and didn't have the motivation to battle for a starting position. And she had a slow arm swing to boot. The problem was that because of some "RMs" (recruiting mistakes) she had to be on the court for us as a junior.

I'll bet I had her in my office every other week of the fall semester trying to find a way to reach her, trying to find a way so she would want to be on the court as much as I wanted her to seize the opportunity. I tried talking to her in the presence of my assistant coach. I tried talking to her one-on-one. I tried e-mail, text messages, and phone calls.

I had her watch scenes from *Dead Poet's Society* where Robin Williams encourages his students to view life through the phrase "carpe diem." No matter what I did, whether I gave her positive encouragement, or when on a few occasions I let her see my frustration with her unwillingness to become (my favorite word) "accountable". . . nothing had an impact.

So I changed my focus. Instead of worrying so much about whether she would ever make the commitment I wanted her to make, I decided to focus on her arm swing. We had a coaches meeting in the war room (the assistant coach's office that used to be the latrine for women's basketball) and we decided to list every possible way we could improve Carrie's ability to terminate as our right-side player.

The first thing we did was change her arm swing from a traditional shoulder rotation to more of a snap arm swing that you see on Asian teams. My thinking was that her wrist and elbow were faster than her shoulder and she would probably contact the ball higher as well.

Then I invited someone from the strength staff to evaluate her attack approach and he noticed that despite her explosive jump she was not very quick off the floor. This was something I knew but hadn't focused on because I was so immersed in trying to solve her arm swing.

We changed her approach so that she planted both feet almost at the same time. This got her off the floor quicker, and combined with a snap arm swing, allowed us to run quicker sets to her. All of her attacks along the net evolved into a quick tempo. She ran a "go" set at left front and a back "shoot set" off serve-receive from right front.

Then we decided to take her out of passing, partly because she had never been an exceptional passer and partly because it would allow her to appear anywhere along the net when she was front row in serve-receive. At the same time, we were trying some other creative ways to speed up her arm swing. Some days we had her attack Wiffle balls. Some days we had her throw footballs like pitchers do in spring training. Three days a week we had her lie down on her stomach, arch her back into extension and throw small medicine balls against the wall.

We built an incline and had her make approaches on it so that she could feel the difference between a slow plant and a quick plant.

Before practice, my assistant coach was trying to teach her to hit shots. After several weeks and three brooms she finally learned to wipe off the block from the right side. But it wasn't until late in her junior year that this shot actually showed up in competition. We almost stopped the match and presented her with the game ball when, two years and three months into her junior year, she finally used the block.

Ben compared it to castling.

By midseason we began to take advantage of her small size by running her on combination plays. Because the rest of our team is relatively tall though unfortunately slow, it was easy for Carrie to get lost among her teammates and come flying out of nowhere to hit a "cross" or "left in." In time, she began to have some success and her attack percentage crept above .200 in late September and it was approaching .300 by early November. With more success on the court, the meetings in my office became fewer and fewer until toward the end of the season we didn't meet at all unless Carrie initiated it (which as you know, a player is not likely to do unless her car or boyfriend blows up).

One day I came into practice and our second assistant was teaching Carrie to miss-hit the ball. I wasn't so sure this was a great idea, especially since we had spent the past two years trying to get her not to hit the ball off the end of her fat fingers. But my assistant explained (in a meeting in my office after practice) that because Carrie didn't have an effective off-speed shot, she thought there might be merit in having her off-speed shot look almost exactly like her regular arm swing. I doubted the logic in this, but at times it's important to encourage a developing assistant coach who is flexing some creative muscles and so I smiled the same way my golden lab smiles at me when she's been sleeping somewhere that she shouldn't.

Well, finally everything came down to the conference tournament. We tied for the conference season championship, but because our power rating is not strong we had to win the conference tournament to be assured of getting a spot in the NCAA, probably opposite Nebraska or Hawaii or Stanford, but that would still be a significant accomplishment for a school that supports women's volleyball and the reforestation of Iraq at about the same level.

We played the Meadowlarks in the first round. They may be the worst team in Division 1 volleyball. Every time they fire their football coach, their volleyball team takes a budget cut. They traveled to the conference tournament in a van and their assistant coach doubles as the trainer and assistant director of admissions. I played our second team in the second and third games and we got out of there without an injury in a match that lasted about an hour.

In the semifinals we played the Lady Armadillos who are a bit unusual in that they run a 5-1 in five rotations and a 6-2 in the sixth rotation. They also have a huge inflatable armadillo that scared the bejeezus out of Ben and everyone else under age 13. It's tough to prepare for the Armadillos because they seem to have a different volleyball philosophy in every rotation. In one game they will make the most brilliant plays and then follow them with an equally dramatic display of self-destruction. Frequently it happens in the same rally. My biggest challenge when we play the "Dillos" (as they refer to themselves) is to not have my team watch them too much. They are so confident in their self-destructiveness that you almost want to join them. It's kind of like watching an entire congregation jump off the roof of a building. It's spectacular and there's an urge to at least walk over to the edge and understand their motivation.

At some point in every game the Dillos are going to lead. They are going to celebrate on every point. They can find something to cheer about in a foot fault. Fortunately, we won 3-1. You just have that feeling if you were out on the court long enough with the Armadillos some of your players might defect.

So that set up our rubber match with the Northeastern Rollers. The Rollers were initially a tiny liberal arts university formed by a small but enthusiastic religious sect in the 19th century, hence, the nickname Holy Rollers. They don't have an inflatable mascot but their "wave" is the best in the conference. And their volleyball team has been the best team in our conference for several years now. They have the best athletes, the most depth, and their coach does an outstanding job preparing them for competition. If the Rollers have an Achilles' heel, it's that sometimes they are over-prepared.

The head coach calls the serves, all the defensive and offensive adjustments, and she does it on every play from a kneeling position three feet from the sideline. If you could substitute on every play, like football teams do, the Rollers would do it. They don't leave anything to chance.

The problem is when they meet a team that has equally gifted athletes outside the Kumquat Valley Conference, and that team does something that the Rollers haven't prepared for, their players have a tendency to look over at the coach with eyes and shoulder shrugs that seem to be saying, "OK, how come you didn't prepare us for this?" But it's hard to take advantage of this flaw if you aren't as athletic or as technically sound as the Rollers. The Rollers usually aren't stressed until they move into the NCAA tournament where they meet teams equal in talent and coaching.

I had the feeling, which I shared with the team, that this was our year. This was the competition that we had been preparing for. We matched up with the Rollers athletically, technically, and mentally. If the Rollers had one advantage, it was in their tradition. They were used to winning the conference tournament, and they were used to beating us on the way.

The first four games went as expected in a kind of dysfunctional way that typifies college volleyball: We were in the zone in game one, having only two unforced errors. We played our best game of the season. We passed, played defense, transitioned, and served tough. It was as if we were a major university playing in primary colors. Final score in game one: Tumbleweeds 15, Rollers 6.

I've always believed that you never want to win the first game by a large margin against a worthy opponent. It's much better to win by two points than nine. Mathematics, psychology, and natural law are all working against you when you defeat a great opponent by too big a margin.

As I anticipated, the Rollers came back with a fury. The tougher they served, the softer we served when we were able to side-out. Because of poor passing we became predictable, and the Rollers' head coach committed her blockers to our outside hitters who were only able to keep the ball in play. I found myself appreciative of how well the Rollers were playing. I would have been disappointed had they responded in any other way. If we were going to win tonight, we would have to beat them at their best.

Games three and four were mirror images of each other. In game three we jumped out to a 9-1 lead and the Rollers fought back to win it 15-12 when we became tentative on our block. In game four the Rollers led 7-2 before we caught them in their weakest rotation, tied them at 9, and went on to win 15-11.

It was a great match. Both teams were playing as well as they could. Several hundred fans supported both schools. The match was televised by a local cable company that gave the players key chains at the tournament banquet. For the first time ever, our athletic director, at the continued prompting of our senior women's administrator, attended the match and I watched her trying to explain the nuances of volleyball to a former football coach.

The game itself came down to one play. With the Tumbleweeds leading 16-15, we served to win our first conference tournament championship. The Rollers set their all-conference middle on a 31 which we dug back up to the setter who had rotated up for the tip. Our middle attacker ran away from the setter as she set a quick back-set to Carrie who was isolated against a single blocker. Suddenly everything turned into slow motion. Carrie planted both feet at the same time and exploded into the air. The Rollers left back player retreated to dig the ball down the line as the middle blocker tried to recover to close the block.

I thought Carrie would snap the ball crosscourt in the hole created by the drifting block, but instead she sped up her arm so that her hand arrived early and the ball came to rest for a brief millisecond on the edge of her fat middle fingers before it softly rebounded just above the blocker's arms. The ball hovered for what seemed like seconds, no, more like minutes, and I could see the expression on the digger's face as she tried to change her momentum when she realized that despite all of her will, all of her training, and all of her athletic ability, she was not prepared for a deliberate miss-hit, and as the ball hit the floor our players were propelled into the air in unison as if we were the last salvo in a Fourth of July celebration.

Within seconds everyone was in a dog pile on the court, including the senior women's administrator and the athletic director and the school mascot "Weedy" who looks more like a disabled cabbage than a tumbleweed, and we were all screaming and crying and the six-piece band was trying to play the fight song without the two-piece brass section which had also become part of the pile, and I was hugging the assistant coach and then hugging the opposing coach . . . and it was wonderful.

Later on the bus trip home, all the players and coaches had fallen asleep, pizza boxes were scattered along the aisles like chrysalises, and the only thing you could hear was this deep, rhythmic breathing, except for the pieces of broken conversation between the bus driver and my assistant coach, who had been assigned to keep him awake.

It was about 1:30 in the morning when Carrie slipped into the seat beside me. This was a first. In all my years as a head coach no upperclassman has ever chosen to ride in the car I was driving, yet alone take a seat next to me on the team bus.

For a long while she didn't say anything and neither did I. But I knew something was coming and after several quiet minutes she said, "Thank you . . . thank you for not giving up." I don't think I have to tell you how delicious it was to hear those words, or how wonderful I felt as she padded back to lay down at the rear of the bus.

For a while I tried to read, but I just kept coming back to this moment where it all seemed worthwhile, and then I decided to write and tell you about it. And that is what I am doing now as this bus, this happy bus, this wonderfully contented bus speeds along the darkness into morning.

TALENT AND THE SECRET LIFE OF TEAMS

While leadership can happen in thousands of ways, there is a tendency for us to see leadership as the lone individual battling an enemy, like Julia Roberts who plays an environmental activist in the movie *Erin Brockovich* or Gary Cooper as the marshal in *High Noon* when he tries to protect Hadleyville from the Miller gang by himself. The heroic individual warrior-leader makes for a wonderful movie, but it is not the most effective blueprint for leadership.

The Captains

In contemporary life leadership is more often collaborative, like the photograph on the cover of this book that was taken from the front of the 1995 University of Nebraska Volleyball Recruiting and Media Guide. Just above the photograph in white type were the words: *One Goal, One Focus, One Champion.*

The women in the photograph are three seniors who were about to embark on their stated goal of winning a national championship for a university that had never achieved that platform in women's volleyball. Not pictured in the photograph were nine other players, three coaches, and hundreds of other people (administrators, mentors, counselors, corporate sponsors, strength coaches, trainers, fans, and custodians) who also played leadership roles in the journey to a national championship.

But the leadership process began with the three women in the photograph who were charged with playing their roles on the volleyball court at an extraordinary level while motivating, challenging, and encouraging their teammates to do likewise. Despite their singleness of purpose, you could not find three more different people in their talents, personalities, and personal tastes.

The player on the left is Billie Winsett, a senior biology major from Booneville, Indiana. Her talent is her will. Her ability to set goals and work toward them until they are accomplished is as natural to her as making a grocery list is to most people. She sewed some of her clothes, raised goats for milk and meat, shoots a musket, and was one of the best serve receivers in college volleyball. She was a straight-A student who had one approach to everything: keep doing it until you get it right, which on rare occasions was frustrating for her teammates when she refused to rotate out of a drill until she dug the ball perfectly to the target. In the spring of her senior year she won the NCAA Woman of the Year Award for her performance on the court coupled with her academic excellence and community service. It is an award that she set out to win by developing a plan and sticking with it.

The player in the middle of the photograph is Christy Johnson, a fifth-year senior setter from Millard, Nebraska. This was *her* team and had been since the beginning of her junior season when she was unanimously selected team captain by her teammates despite the fact she spent the previous three years either as a substitute or, during one season, a redshirt.

She had overcome more challenges than anyone else on the team to become a great player. For two years she battled Nikki Stricker, another talented setter, for the starting position and lost it, not because she wasn't a better player but because in a program built on leveraging talent, Nikki was more effective setting the team's dominant attacker. It would be like a great point guard losing the starting position because another guard could get the ball to LeBron James more effectively. Christy considered quitting or transferring because of the exhaustive competitive battle she faced, but each time she returned with a stronger commitment to make herself a better player. Her teammates trusted her because of how she overcame the challenges.

What they didn't know were the doubts and fears she had about her ability to perform under pressure that she wrote about in her journal. She had the quality that all great leaders possess—the ability to be afraid and then set her fear aside and act courageously.

The player on the right side of the photograph is Allison Weston, a senior from Papillion, Nebraska, who was the best all-around player in the history of Nebraska Volleyball. She was a middle attacker who led the country in attack percentage and blocks per game while also serving as a primary passer. She was shy, polite, and thoughtful almost to a fault. If she made a mistake on the court she tugged on the collar of her uniform and swore to herself inside the shirt. She majored in forestry, and on the occasion that she had time to herself, took off with her bass rod to a local lake. Her long-term goal was to be a forest ranger in a national park. Her short-term goal, like the other two women in the photo, was to do everything possible to lead Nebraska Volleyball to a national championship. Allison led with her physical presence, her athleticism, and her willingness to support Christy Johnson in Christy's role as the director of the team on the court.

After graduating from Nebraska, Allison became captain of the U.S. Olympic women's volleyball team while playing as an outside hitter, a position she didn't play in college. She and the other two senior captains each earned a perfect 4.0 grade point average in their final semester competing for Nebraska Volleyball.

The cover photograph of the three players in practice gear is an unusual context for a media guide cover, which can include everything from evening gowns to Maseratis and bazookas. The countenance of the players does not have the false *pissed off* look that is sometimes coupled with military garb and armament. It is simple and direct. Three players have finished practicing with a purpose. They look the camera in the eye, not with disdain or anger at the interruption, but as if you caught them by surprise in a routine that takes place every day for them: practicing and preparing to compete for a national championship. When I saw the photograph for the first time, it had a dramatic effect on me. It was like a public announcement that our intent is to win the national championship. It was a goal that we would now have to hold ourselves accountable to.

A Mentoring Team

Looking backward, it is easy for me to identify other transformational moments in the 1995 season that would be critical to our success. One of the most important took place late in the season when I made a phone call to David Cook.

Dr. David Cook is an author, sports psychologist, Christian speaker, mentor, father, husband, and a fellow avid golfer and fly-fisherman. We met at a sports clinic in Lincoln in the summer of 1995 and became fast friends. I asked David to present to our team on the challenges of trying to win a national championship during two-a-day practices in mid-August 1995. He spent several hours interacting with the players and coaches in a workshop designed to lay a foundation of trust and a willingness to embrace great expectations.

David became a member of my peer-mentoring team that included Frank Brown, a close friend and clinical social worker, and John Cook, then the head women's volleyball coach at the University of Wisconsin. There was no formal contract between these three people and me, other than they were friends whom I trusted and spoke with regularly either over lunch or by telephone.

Each person provided unique insights that I thought would help me make better decisions as a potential championship season unfolded. John Cook had been my assistant coach from 1988 to 1990 before leaving to become the assistant coach on the U.S. Men's National Team. He became the head coach at Wisconsin following the Barcelona Olympics, and he was in the process of building a program that eventually won a Big 10 Championship and advanced to the NCAA Final Four.

My conversations with John were volleyball-specific. We talked about systems, strategy, tactical decisions, and bounced ideas off each other about the challenges we were facing. I felt it was important to interact with someone outside my program who understood coaching volleyball.

Frank Brown is a personal counselor who became a close friend. He had the ability to identify the developmental issues of the players I was coaching and help me devise the healthiest way to coach them. Sometimes he came to practices and watched the behaviors I described and then suggested a way I could help the player move through a crisis that had temporarily stalled her development. Each of these three people—John Cook, Frank Brown, and David Cook—had a significant impact on my coaching decisions during the 1995 season.

The Phone Call

When I called David Cook in mid-November 1995, it was to ask him a very specific question. We were having a tremendous season with a team that had great leadership from three seniors. With the exception of an early loss to defending national champion Stanford, we had won every match, most of them without losing a game, and we were continuing to get better as the season progressed. Still, I had an uneasy feeling as we moved toward the beginning of the NCAA tournament.

Five of our starters were typical Nebraska Volleyball student athletes. They were from the Midwest, (four within a six-hour drive from Lincoln), exceptional students, and technically very efficient with their volleyball skills. Four of them would receive All-American recognition. Billie Winsett became NCAA Woman of the Year, Allison Weston was co-winner of the Honda Broderick Award as the outstanding college volleyball player of 1995, and the setter, Christy Johnson, led Nebraska to a 62-2 record in her junior and senior years while never losing an away match.

Lisa Reitsma, a sophomore right-side player earned All-American honors her final three seasons, and a fifth starter, Jen McFadden, the middle blocker who played opposite Weston, was one of the most intimidating blockers in college volleyball. We also had an exceptional defensive specialist, Maria Hedbeck, a junior from Sollentuna, Sweden.

It was the sixth starter that I had concerns about. Her name was Kate Crnich and she didn't look like or execute fundamentals like any other Husker. Kate was from Chicago's West Side and was somewhat of an enigma. Six feet tall with dark black hair (in contrast to the dishwater blondes who live in Nebraska and western Iowa), she wore tight black leather pants on her recruiting visit and professed a love for a punk rock group, "The Ramones," who were not likely to make an appearance in Lincoln any time soon.

Kate was a good but not great student who majored in gerontology at a time when many college students did not even want to be in a room with someone over 30. She not only did not have a car, she had never driven a car and did not anticipate that she would ever need to do so. There was some irony in this in that she was attending a land grant university where it is not unusual for kids on farms and ranches to drive when they're 13. But that wasn't what differentiated Kate the most from her teammates. In a volleyball program that prided itself on teaching fundamentals, where every player executed athletic movements in a trained and disciplined manner, Kate was inefficient in all of her movements. She was *goofy-footed,* meaning that she closed with the wrong foot when she attacked. She passed serves while jumping backward and hovering 3 inches above the court. She may have been the least analytical player I had ever coached, requiring one of her teammates, senior team co-captain Billie Winsett, to keep her informed about which of the opponent's hitters were eligible attackers when we were serving. Billie also shepherded her into the correct base defense we were playing and generally managed some of Kate's on-court decisions.

So why was Kate on the court? Because she was also very talented. She played exceptional defense, and despite passing with one or two feet airborne, she was a very good passer. She could hit the daylights out of the ball, although one feared that if she did so for very long while closing on the wrong foot she would eventually blow out her shoulder. Fortunately, on a team that led the country in attack percentage, Kate was the fifth option of five attackers and so she was unlikely to ever receive enough sets to strain, let alone damage, her shoulder.

What was more frustrating than her fundamental deficiencies was that I was spending a considerable amount of time trying to fix her. Every day before practice she would come in and I worked with her posture and balance on serve so that by the time practice began, she looked like she could be a cousin to the other players on the court. But if we missed one day of individual work on her serve, she resorted to a flailing scramble that could best described as a beautiful woman falling down a staircase, and out of this tumbling mass would come a weak serve to the middle of the opponent's court, giving them a great opportunity to side-out.

When I closed my eyes, it was hard for me to envision Nebraska winning a national championship with a player on the court who was so different from our brand. This bothered me for several days before I called my friend David Cook and told him about the nightmares I was having.

David listened as I outlined my concerns about Kate, and then asked if I had any other options. "I have two freshmen who are going to be great players," I said. "One is an outside hitter named Jamie Krondak, who has the fundamental skills to play right now but I question whether she is emotionally mature enough to handle the assignment. The coaching staff hoped she would win the position by mid-season but it hasn't happened. The other freshman, Fiona Nepo, is a warrior — a 'Samoan Warrior'— as she likes to remind me, who could handle the mental challenges of playing for a national championship, but is being trained as a setter and doesn't have any experience as an outside hitter. With six weeks of very specific training she might be ready, but we don't have six weeks."

David listened and then he responded, "Well if that's the case, here's where I think you're at. You could continue to train the two freshmen as options that you might have to go to, but I think your best bet is to approach Kate in a different way. When you meet with her before the next practice, you could tell her that you aren't going to work on her serve or change her footwork on attack. Tell her that she's already good enough and that she will be on the court when Nebraska wins the national championship."

As David spoke I knew he was right. After two and half years of training, Kate wasn't going to change anything that she hadn't changed by now. She also was our best option. She was a good player, probably a better player than I was acknowledging. David was speaking to me more than he was speaking about Kate. He was saying I needed to recognize her value even though it might be packaged differently than our other players, and that her best chance to play well was if I embraced who she was rather than try to change her.

Later that day I went to the Coliseum and waited for Kate to walk up and begin our daily serving fix. When she arrived I quoted David almost verbatim, ending with the phrase, "Kate, you're good enough as you are. Forget all the technical stuff. You'll be on the court when we win the national championship." I may have fudged a bit by imagining that my fingers were crossed behind my back, but I believed that the message David suggested was our best chance for success.

In the two weeks leading up to the NCAA tournament, we continued to play well, winning the Big 8 Championship easily while focusing on our strengths and preparing for the teams we believed we could meet deep in the NCAA tournament. Kate no longer received any remedial work, and Christy made a concerted effort to set Kate more when we were in system in practice, something we had not done for most of the season. Because our passing and ball handling were so strong, Christy almost always had her choice of options and usually fed the ball to our dominant middle attackers, Jen McFadden and Allison Weston, or 6-foot-4-inch Lisa Reitsma who had developed into one of the most effective opposite attackers in the country.

Our two outside hitters usually received sets in transition when we were out of system or when teams committed on our quick attackers. Kate, in particular, would get a dozen sets each match when we mishandled the ball and were forced to set a high ball to the left side. Billie Winsett, the other left-side player, had developed a repertoire of off-speed and placement shots that meant she *did* receive some sets in system. To this point in the season, Weston and Reitsma averaged four to five kills a game while McFadden and Winsett averaged three. Crnich averaged one and a half kills per game, barely more than our setter averaged on tips and dumps.

The NCAA Tournament

When the NCAA tournament began, Nebraska hosted George Mason in the first round and defeated the Patriots in three games, 15-2, 15-5, 16-14. The box score reveals a match where the Huskers distributed the ball more evenly, with Kate Crnich having five kills, slightly more than her season average. There was nothing unusual about the match that served as a prelude to much stronger competition the following weekend when Nebraska met regional rival Penn State and national power UCLA in NCAA Regional matches hosted in the NU Coliseum.

Nebraska defeated Penn State in four games 15-7, 15-6, 14-16, 15-2. The match had an edge to it because Penn State had defeated Nebraska in a tough regional final the previous year. That had been a much more experienced Penn State team, and some of their key players had graduated. When I looked at the box score following the match, Kate Crnich had thirteen kills, a career high. I remember thinking that our decision to stop trying to fix Kate seemed to be working.

The emphasis on distributing the ball more evenly and setting our left-side players more often in system was also reaping benefits. While Kate's fundamentals in attack, passing, and serving looked the same, she was beginning to develop the confidence that a player gets when she senses the setter and her coaches have confidence in her as well.

UCLA figured to be a tougher test, not just because the Bruins were historically one of the best teams in the country, but because West Coast teams traditionally had better ball handling than the strongest Midwest teams.

Ball handling and defense had been our primary focuses for the past year. In the spring I sent my associate head coach, Cathy Noth, to Long Beach State, which I considered to be the best passing and floor defense team in the country. Forty-niner head coach Brian Gimmillaro welcomed Cathy and allowed her to watch practice, take notes, and ask as many questions as she wanted. When she returned we adopted some of the technical aspects of the Long Beach defense and adapted others. Most importantly, we made a decision that the first thirty-five minutes of every practice would be dedicated to individual defense with each player digging over a hundred balls thrown by her partner to very specific positions.

UCLA head coach Andy Banachowski knew that the Huskers, who were ranked No. 1 in the country, would be athletic with strong setting, attacking and blocking, but he did not know that Nebraska had developed into one of the best defensive teams in the country. After the match, which the Huskers won 15-9, 15-7, 16-14, he relayed that message to reporters: "Nebraska was much stronger defensively than we anticipated. They are a great team."

One of our strategies against UCLA was to slow down their All-American middle attacker, Kim Krull, who I had tried unsuccessfully to recruit to Nebraska. UCLA ran a very quick middle set to Krull that required the opposing team to commit on the block before the setter released the ball.

I have a theory that players, particularly setters, tend to imprint the first few plays of a match into patterns. In other words, if your team tries to take away a specific attack from the opponent early and you are successful, there is a tendency for the opposing setter to believe that you are continuing with that tactic throughout the match even though you aren't. I did not want the UCLA setter to be comfortable setting Krull, who besides being a dynamic attacker was a very passionate player who could rally her teammates on an opponent's court. The decision to commit to Krull early seemed to be successful because we held her to eleven kills and a .056 attack percentage. But what was even more important was a Nebraska defense that combined seventeen blocks and fifty-three digs to hold the Bruins to a team attack percentage of .167. Weston and Reitsma combined for thirty-four kills to provide more than enough offense to send the Huskers on to the Final Four in Amherst, Massachusetts.

The Championship Semifinals

The 1995 Championship finals at the University of Massachusetts was one of the first Final Fours to feature four teams that each had a legitimate chance to win. The fact that the four teams were from different regions of the country in a sport that had been dominated by West Coast teams also created an air of anticipation.

Stanford, which was seeded No. 1, was the defending champion and featured two All-American setters, Cary Wendell and Lisa Sharpley, plus Kristin Fokl, the most physically dominant left-side player in college volleyball. Stanford had all-stars at every position and a few on the bench as well, which can sometimes create other problems.

Nebraska was seeded No. 2 and Western Regional winner Michigan State, coached by Chuck Erbe, was seeded No. 3 with a 34-2 record. Texas, coached by Mick Haley, had experienced a unique season, losing its first three matches of the year before following the lead of its All-American setter, Carrie Busch, and an overpowering freshman outside hitter, Demetria Sance, to upset a great Florida team in the

Southeast Regional in Gainesville.

Nebraska met Michigan State in the first semifinal in the early afternoon at the Mullins Center on the UMass campus on a Wallace Stevens kind of day: *It was snowing and it was going to snow.* Michigan State was a very balanced team with All-Conference or All-American players at every position and great leadership from its senior setter, Courtney DeBolt.

While we had developed a game plan for the Spartans, I had thought Hawaii, not Michigan State, would advance out of the Western Regional. Michigan State was a tough matchup because they did some unique things on offense that required very specific preparation. Their best all-around player, Dana Cooke, was a middle blocker who also passed when she was in the front row and would swing to several different zones along the net to attack at a variety of tempos. Val Sterk was the best blocker in the Big 10 and the combination of Veronica Morales and Jenna Wrobel gave Michigan State one of the best left-side tandems in the tournament.

Nebraska was tight at the beginning of the match and lost the first game 15-10 before recovering to win games two and three with identical 15-8 scores by holding the Spartan hitters to an attack percentage of less than .120. Michigan State won the fourth game 15-9, and after four games the statistics revealed how even the match was. Both teams were attacking in the mid-.200s. Nebraska had a slight lead in kills while Michigan State had seven fewer service errors. Both setters were distributing the ball to their strengths. The Spartans' outside hitters, Wrobel and Morales, accumulated seventeen kills apiece on the outside and the Spartans All-American middle blockers, Dana Cooke and Val Sterk, earned eleven and twelve kills each from the middle and Corrie Richard earned ten from the right side.

Nebraska played to its strengths as well. Allison Weston got thirty kills flying from pin to pin while Billie Winsett had nineteen kills from the left side, many of them in endgame. Lisa Reitsma added eighteen kills from the right side of the court and Jen McFadden contributed twelve kills and five blocks. Reitsma and McFadden would be involved in a play that would become one of the defining moments for Nebraska volleyball and my career as a coach.

When Morales hit a ball off the Nebraska block to tie the score at seven in the fifth game, there was an automatic television time-out. As the team gathered in front of the bench, I walked toward the huddle thinking about the issues I wanted to share with them before they returned to the court. For the first time in my coaching career, there really was nothing to say. Both teams had played well and hard, both coaches had made the appropriate adjustments. From here on, it would be a players' match, and so I was surprised as I walked into the huddle to find myself saying:

"There is one thing that I want you to know. I love you. And my love for you is not dependent upon you winning this game."

It was unlike any huddle that I had ever been a part of. It was not something that I had planned to say, or even dreamed of saying. Christy Johnson started crying. Allison Weston and Billie Winsett started laughing, not at Christy, but at the context of what was happening. Here in the most important, and perhaps the last time-out of their collegiate careers, their coach, who has a propensity to analyze everything, offers no technical or strategic advice, but instead says something that he has never said to any of them before. Even as I was saying *"I love you"* it was as if I was watching someone else speaking and I, like everyone else, was astounded.

After we regrouped and Christy wiped her face with a Kleenex, we returned to the court to await the serve from the Michigan State setter, Courtney DeBolt. On the next play, Christy set Lisa Reitsma a back set while Jen McFadden ran a quick approach for a middle attack. Reitsma hit the ball into a solid block set by Sterk and Morales. As the ball fell to the floor the 6-foot-2-inch McFadden, who had just landed from her own approach, turned and dove back toward the 10-foot line and scooped the ball with a fist just inches from the floor, where it rose in slow tumbling motion over the net, over the celebrating Spartans, and fell into the opposite corner for a side-out.

It was an unbelievably athletic play that only happens once in a career and only then if an athlete is playing without any hesitation or fear. It deflated the Spartans as much as it energized the Huskers who then outscored Michigan State eight points to one to win the final game, 15-8. After a very brief celebration and meeting in the locker room we

136

returned to the court to watch the other semifinal match to determine who our opponent would be in the finals the day after tomorrow.

I didn't reflect on how I came to say what I said to the team in the final time-out until much later. It wasn't something I planned to say, and it would have created interference if the team believed that the words weren't true. I do believe it was a message that may have relaxed the players as they returned to the court and enabled them to play without fear.

We needed to scout the next match, review video that we had accumulated on the winning team, and come up with a game plan. We would have a two-hour practice the next day and a one-hour practice before the match on Saturday morning. I anticipated that Stanford would most likely win the other semifinal because they were very talented, deep, and experienced. They also would be the hardest team for Nebraska to prepare for because we had played Texas three weeks earlier and much of the scouting and preparation would be done if we played the Longhorns.

Stanford presented some unique problems because they ran a two-setter system that sometimes morphed into a 5-1 with Lisa Sharpely or Cary Wendell setting in transition from the front row. We would have to find a way to slow down Fokl and be alert enough to adjust to Stanford's ability to move between systems while continuing to do what we do best. I fully anticipated that we would play Stanford as I sat in the end zone behind my first volleyball coach, Jim Coleman, the 1968 men's Olympic coach.

But Texas coach Mick Haley had other things in mind. Mick had made an unusual coaching decision during the Stanford match that was having positive results. After the second game, which Texas lost 0-15, he removed himself from the huddle during time-outs and allowed his team to gather by themselves and make adjustments in a collaborative dialogue. I've never seen anything like it before or since, but it was absolutely the right thing to do because it was working. I suspect Mick sensed that one or two of his upperclassmen had stopped listening and so he resorted to the only option he had. By removing himself from the huddle, he gave the team one less reason not to do something.

Texas went on to upset Stanford in five games despite losing the second game 0-15, something that rarely happens in developmental volleyball, let alone an NCAA Division 1 semifinal. I remember watching the match and feeling that there were elements of Muhammad Ali's "rope-a-dope" tactics the great boxer used against George Foreman in the heavyweight championship fight in Zaire. Like Ali, Texas was overmatched physically. To have any chance, Texas had to change the tempo and psychological dynamics of the match. Coach Haley attempted to do this by continually serving short against a Stanford team that was running a 6-2 offense with three front-row hitters.

Most coaches will refrain from serving short when the opponent has three front-row attackers because the serve is easy to pass, and even if it slows down one of the hitters, the setter still has two options off a pass that is no more difficult than a free ball. But Texas continued to serve short even after being skunked in the second game. One of the by-products of serving short is that it gives the setter a lot of time to think about her options. In effect, when a setter has too much time she can become overly analytical and begin to think her way through a match instead setting from feel.

A lot of variables had to be aligned for Texas to win the match. Player for player, Stanford had better talent and more experience. But a strange thing happened. As the match evolved, Stanford's setters, Carrie Wendel and Lisa Sharpley, began setting each other more frequently instead of setting Fokl and Stanford's other All-American hitters. The match seemed as if it was being played in slow motion, almost like a match race at a velodrome where two cyclists stop and start and stop again until one of them can gain an advantage.

In the end, Stanford felt the pressure that a professional baseball player must feel when he faces a knuckle ball pitcher throwing the ball at sixty-five miles an hour. You are supposed to win this. You won it last year and all the key players are back. But there is also another saying in sport: *Less talent means less baggage.* While the Longhorns may have had some mental challenges, Coach Haley had effectively negated those by removing himself as an obstacle. He had also given his team a chance to win by tactically slowing the game down, giving the Stanford team time to think. Texas rope-a-doped Stanford and won the match 15-13, 0-15, 15-17, 15-6, 15-12. I remember watching the match as it played out and thinking, "Lord have mercy, we are going to play Texas not Stanford, and while they will be a motivated and difficult opponent, it's going to require less video and preparation time. We can do this."

Preparing to Win

I was wrong. The difference between playing against a great opponent and playing against a great opponent for a national championship is the difference between walking across a creek on a plank and walking across a creek on a plank at 14,000 feet. Despite having coached in two previous championship matches, there is nothing in women's intercollegiate volleyball that can prepare you and your team for the opportunities for interference in both preparation and execution.

The All-American banquet traditionally takes place at noon on the day between the semifinal matches and the championship match. For the two teams in the finals it can be a potential land mine if you have a player who is more focused on individual awards or the perceived slights of not being recognized. Fortunately, because our senior leadership of Johnson, Weston, and Winsett was focused on only one goal, it was not a distraction for our team.

I understand why the AVCA hosts the banquet to recognize All-Americans from all levels of intercollegiate volleyball, but it is a potentially lethal distraction for the two teams who will play for the national championship the next day. I have seen players who could not get past the fact that someone else on their team earned an award that they felt entitled to, and it impacted the play in the championship match. I know of some coaches who feel so strongly about the potential interference that they have come close to not having their team or honorees attend the banquet.

The biggest challenge for a coach is a combination of fatigue and the enormity of the opportunity before you. The mental and physical exhaustion of coaching your way through the NCAA first and second rounds, the NCAA regional, and championship semifinals can almost create a situation where you want to sleep rather than continue to prepare. But you can't do that. And so you watch a video on the opponent for the fifth and sixth time, trying to pick up a potential vulnerability or pattern that might be useful in the championship match.

On the eve of the championship I spent the late evening and early morning in my room with Wisconsin coach John Cook talking about the upcoming match. John was offering more emotional support than tactical insight. He was not nearly as familiar with Texas as I was, with Nebraska having defeated the Longhorns just a few weeks earlier in Austin. At about three o'clock in the morning as he stumbled off to his own room, John said something that would have an important impact on how I prepared my team for the match. He said, "Did you notice that Christy's sets were dying inside the pin against Michigan State?" I replied that I hadn't, but that we could make that adjustment in the one-hour practice in the morning.

A volleyball coach's seat on the bench is one of the worst places to watch a match. If you sit on the end of the bench nearest the scorer's table you can't tell whether the block is solid or the sets are precise. You can see major errors but not the slight variations in tempo and geometry that can make the difference in a successful attack or a blocked ball. It is one of the reasons that I would frequently walk down to the end of the bench and stand by the substitutes while getting a cup of water.

Somehow I had missed the observation John made about Christy's sets during the Michigan State match, possibly because we were forcing the ball to our middle attackers and right-side player so much. Weston, McFadden, and Reitsma had combined for more than 130 attacks. I appreciated John's observation and as I fell asleep for three hours I dreamt about the ramifications of trap setting our left-side hitters.

When I awoke a game plan had formulated in my mind. When two teams of equal talent meet for the second time, the team that lost the first match is at an advantage because the adjustments they need to make are more obvious. When Nebraska had played Texas in November our middle attackers, Weston and McFadden, had great success on quick attacks and Reitsma had been unstoppable from behind the setter. Mick Haley was too experienced to not address these issues. I anticipated that he might place his blockers in the middle of the net to try and slow down our middles and right side and defend our outside hitters with one blocker if need be. I believed he probably thought Texas could not beat us by defending our two middle attackers and right-side player straight up. If Texas followed this strategy, I anticipated it would be disastrous if Christy's sets died inside where our outside attackers could not take advantage of Texas's bunch blocking.

Because of an impending snowstorm I had moved the team from a hotel in Springfield to some rooms on top of the student center on the UMass campus in Amherst. I did not want the stress of having a half-hour commute turn into a two-hour bus ride before practicing and playing a national championship match. It may have been one of the best coaching decisions I ever made. It was snowing hard on Saturday morning before our last practice, but as we walked down the hill to the arena the players were relaxed and rested, throwing snowballs at each other and seemingly energized by a storm that could have created unnecessary anxiety if we were bussing from Springfield.

At the morning practice we reviewed our blocking and serving schemes for each rotation, but we spent a majority of our time having Christy set quick-tempo balls to our outside hitters and making sure that the sets were still rising when then they reached the antenna. We had Crnich and Winsett practice attacking against a unique Texas defense where the right-side blocker would give the line and the right-back digger would rotate up for the tip. This required the Texas middle-back defender to rotate all the way to the corner to dig a ball hit down the line.

While I had not talked with Mick about his defense, I thought it was based on two premises. One was statistically based and the other was based on Texas's personnel and strengths. If the right-side blocker gave line it required less time and effort for the Texas middles to close the block and statistically, left-side attackers hit more balls crosscourt than to other areas of the court.

By encouraging opponents to try to attack the line, the Texas defense also was using the sideline similar to the way a basketball team tries to force a dribbler out of bounds. It limits your options and there is more potential for error. It also allowed Texas's two strongest attackers, outside All-American hitters Demetria Sance and Angie Breitenfield, to be in position to transition without having to come across the court to play a tip.

141

There was one other advantage to Haley's defense. Because Texas was the only team that ran what amounted to a hybrid-rotation defense, it required everyone who played the Longhorns to prepare for something different, and that is always a tactical advantage if the adaptation matches your personnel.

In the early afternoon the team had its pre-match meal at an Italian restaurant a couple of blocks from campus. It was a relaxed atmosphere with parents and our biggest fan, Dr. Barbara Hibner, the senior women's administrator, joining us for the meal. Anne and our oldest daughter, Katherine, were there as well. Katherine was a junior setter on a high school team that had been ranked No. 1 in the country only to lose its final match to a team it had beaten four times during the regular season. That fact was not lost on either of us.

After the meal Katherine and I ran through the streets of Amherst in foot-deep snow following the tracks of delivery trucks back to the student center where I began dressing for the match. Katherine spent time during the match painting the faces of Husker fans with NU VB. Katherine, perhaps more than anyone else, sensed how important this match was to me personally. When her team lost the championship match to end her season, she woke up in the middle of the night and came up to our bedroom in tears mumbling words about having made the wrong setting choice at a critical point in the match. This is a truth that everyone I know who has ever taken great risks in the competitive arena knows. The pain of losing when you feel you were in position to win is far greater than the joy of winning.

More than any match against a great opponent that I have ever coached, I felt confident in our chances against Texas. We were prepared. Not just for this match, but we had prepared ourselves to be in this arena for the past three years. Three years earlier I had pulled Johnson, Winsett, and Weston aside during practice and told them that they would all be on the court in significant roles when Nebraska won its first national championship. At the time, only Weston was a starter. I am not sure what they made of that pronouncement or whether they even remembered it. But one thing I've learned over the years in coaching is that it can't happen if the coach doesn't believe it and if he isn't willing to say it.

The other reason I was able to coach out of a quiet confidence instead of fear was because of the great passion and leadership of our setter, Christy Johnson. More than any player I had ever coached, she had been through a crucible of competition, disappointment, fear and, at last, courage.

Christy had been recruited one year behind Nikki Stricker, a great athlete from Lincoln, Nebraska, who would become MVP of the Big 8 conference, a three-time starter at the setter position, and team captain. Nikki probably had as much natural talent as any setter I ever coached. Christy took a great risk in accepting a scholarship in a class one year behind Nikki. For two years they competed for the starting position knowing that both of them were among the best setters in the country. Nikki won the position both years even though Christy might have been the better all-around setter.

The competition eventually wore both players out, and in an effort to set up the best possible chance for a national championship in 1995, I redshirted Christy in 1993, Nikki's senior season. That decision more than any other was the reason we were in position to win a national championship. In the span of two years Christy became a vocal leader even though that was not natural for her. She played with emotion, not for herself, but because I asked her to do it. If someone is playing with passion and celebrating positive plays, it is very difficult for other players to turn inward and become self-absorbed. Throughout the 1995 tournament run she slapped more teammates on the back and offered more words of encouragement than a congressman running for re-election. And she did it not because it was natural to her, but because she was asked to do so.

For the last two seasons I had asked her to hold her teammates accountable. She did so by throwing a player out of a drill when she thought the effort was not appropriate to the team's goal. For the first half of the 1995 season she took it as a personal mission to teach Lisa Reitsma, our gifted sophomore right-side player, to be mentally tough. She did it by putting Lisa in pit drills when she didn't go for the ball; she did it by barking at her when her effort was less than great. It took her two years to learn how to do this in a way that helped to develop character without breaking down team chemistry.

143

It culminated one evening in late November when Christy was lifting weights in the training room and Lisa and another freshman, Stacie Maser, were the only other volleyball players left in the strength center. The two freshmen heard someone crying, looked over and saw Christy on the bench press with tears in her eyes. When they walked over and asked what the problem was, Christy responded:

"I want you guys to know that me holding you responsible every day is the hardest thing I've ever had to do in my life. But I also want you to know that winning a national championship at Nebraska is the most important thing to me, and I will continue to do it."

I did not learn of this interaction until years later. Many of the most important elements to a championship season occur during the secret life of teams that coaches are not privy to. That is when you really need leadership. We can train behaviors, we can create a culture that works hard and develops sound fundamentals, but we can only encourage someone to lead when we are out of the room.

Situations arise that we cannot even imagine in which the balance of a season may turn on what is said between two players. Much of the confidence that I had in our team was in the courageous decisions our setter would make and the support she drew from her two senior classmates, Weston and Winsett, who provided leadership in other ways–Weston with her physical presence and Winsett with her unfailingly consistent play and will. (If Winsett missed passing a ball perfectly her senior year, I do not remember it.) It was not so much that I was sure we would win the national championship match as was my feeling that if I ever fell short of achieving something I really wanted, this is the team I wanted to go down with.

I had packed a suit for the championship match but, much to Anne's consternation, decided to wear a sweater and an older pair of shoes that I felt were lucky. I thought the most important thing I could do to prepare myself for the match was to be comfortable. And something unexpected happened just before the match that helped contribute to that.

Fiona Nepo was our freshman backup setter. Her mother, Sunita, had traveled to the match from their home in Honolulu, Hawaii. As I was about to take my place on the bench, Sunita placed a purple lei around my neck and told me that she had a dream about me wearing the exact sweater I had chosen for the match. I shared Sunita's dream with Anne later on to justify my decision not to wear a suit.

The Final Match

The arena was not packed because of the snowstorm, but there was a good crowd of over 7,300 people, many of them Husker fans who were having their faces painted by the coach's daughter. Lil' Red, Nebraska's inflatable mascot, entertained the crowd by bouncing on his head, and small pep bands from both schools alternated playing the Nebraska and Texas fight songs. It was the first time that two non-West Coast schools had ever met in a championship match, and both of the teams would be in the newly formed Big 12 conference the following year. If Nebraska won, we would be the first Midwest team to do so. If Texas won, it would be a great achievement for a team that appeared to be foundering when the season began. It might also start a movement for *no coach* huddles.

With the exception of Kate Crnich, Nebraska was slow out of the gate in game one of the 1995 National Championship match. The Huskers committed five service errors and eleven attack errors. Crnich recorded eight kills in game one as did Texas freshman outside hitter Demetria Sance, who was a force attacking the ball down the line. The Huskers were tight and made too many unforced errors. Texas got off to an early 10-3 lead before winning the first game, 15-11. Nebraska had twenty-one kills to Texas's thirteen, but committed several more attack errors. The Texas game plan of committing its middle blockers on Weston had an impact. Allison, a traditionally low-error attacker, had six attack errors in game one.

Texas was running a rotation defense but giving the line to Nebraska's left-side hitters so that the Longhorns' right-side blockers, setter Carrie Busch and opposite Katie Austin, could help on quick sets to Weston and McFadden. Crnich benefited from the bunch blocking as the majority of her kills landed two-thirds of the way down the line in front of the Texas middle-back player who rotated to the corner. Texas was committing its blockers to Nebraska's strength and slowing down the Huskers' middle and right-side attackers. Whether Nebraska could adjust to the Longhorns' strategy and attack the weakness in their defense would determine the outcome of the match.

For the next two and a half games Nebraska dominated the match, outscoring the Longhorns 39 to 12, winning games two and three decisively and taking a 9-3 lead in game four.

The Huskers did so with Christy Johnson distributing the ball equally to her five attackers and setting left-side players Winsett and Crnich in system instead of forcing the ball to the middle attackers and the Texas block. Crnich and Winsett combined for fifty kills, twenty-five each, both of them career highs. In the middle of game three during a time-out Christy Johnson pulled me aside and asked if we should continue pushing the ball to Kate and Billie. I remembered a plaque hanging on the kitchen wall of Frank Brown, the clinical social worker who was part of my mentoring team. The plaque read: *Ride the horse in the direction it's going.*

There is a strong temptation to resort to what has typically worked in the past under stress. It took a good deal of courage to tell her to keep feeding our outside attackers and trust that they could keep up their success. I don't know that I could have made that decision if I had not recalled the plaque in Frank's kitchen or outlined a season of trust based on conversations with David Cook. The game plan we were following was partly the result of John Cook's observation that Christy's sets were falling short in the Michigan State match. The success that Billie Winsett and Kate Crnich were having on the outside was in part due to the conversation with John two days before the match.

Despite dominating the second game 15-2, winning the third game 15-7, and opening up a 9-3 lead in game four, it did not *feel* like we were dominating the match. Some of that is because of the importance of the match. No matter how well a team is playing in a national championship match, a coach is never comfortable until the match is over and his team has won three games. It was also the nature of side-out volleyball, where a team has to be playing better volleyball than the opponent at the end of the match to win. In today's rally score version of volleyball, a team can build up a five-point lead and coast to victory by siding out. Because there are no points awarded for siding out, the games in side-out volleyball between two great teams can also take considerably longer. The winning team may trade several side-outs in a row with the opponent before earning a point. No matter how far ahead your team is, you feel as though you are never out of the woods.

In the national championship match, Nebraska had 101 kills to 62 for Texas. Despite the disparity in the statistic that most accurately reveals a team's performance, the match was still in doubt until Allison Weston and Christy Johnson combined for a stuff block on Demetria Sance to win the fourth game, 16-14.

Both teams had eleven blocks. Nebraska hit .296 for the match and Texas hit .193, but if Demetria Sance had hit for a kill on what became the last play of the match, Texas would have served to tie the fourth game and possibly force a fifth game where the pressure and psychological dynamics are difficult to prepare for. It would be an actuarial nightmare to try to determine how each team would play in the fifth game.

When the block hit the floor and the referee, Verna Klubikin, signaled the match was over I threw my clipboard to the sky, then immediately worried it might hit someone. While the Huskers formed the traditional dog pile on the court, I saw Dr. Hibner approach the bench with T-shirts declaring the University of Nebraska Volleyball team the 1995 National Champions. Unbeknownst to me, the booster club had the T-shirts printed and had printed similar shirts in 1989 only to have the Huskers routed in the championship final by Long Beach State. As I understand it, those shirts were shipped to a relief effort in China where there still may be Chinese farmworkers wearing them today.

I motioned to Dr. Hibner not to bring out the shirts. You would have to be in a position to lose a national championship to know why I waved the T-shirts away. There is nothing so painful as putting yourself in the national championship match and then not having success. Texas had played a great tournament. They deserved better than to have our players wearing T-shirts that implied we were so confident that we had them printed before the championship. I know there are a lot of coaches and fans who might disagree with me, but I've always believed that the most important thing in competition is to have a worthy opponent who is as talented, well coached, and well prepared as you are.

Texas met all those criteria and I wanted them to know we understood that. I wanted our players to honor the game, not just their success in the game.

The Box Score

Statistics don't always tell the story, but in this case, they did. Nebraska's first NCAA National Championship in women's volleyball was a collaborative effort.

• Kate Crnich and Billie Winsett combined for fifty kills from the outside hitter position, both career highs. Crnich's achievement received more recognition than Winsett's because it was so unexpected. The Amherst newspaper ran the following headline the day after the match: "The Crnich That Stole Christmas." They achieved their kills in different ways. Crnich pounded the ball down the line and took advantage of the Texas strategy to bunch block in the middle. Winsett attacked the ball into the seams of a rotation defense while applying more wrist than usual to her attacks. The ball looked the same to the digger, but fell 2 or 3 feet short of where the digger was positioned. Crnich hit .500 for the match and for a while some volleyball wags came up with the theory that the most important variable in a championship match is the performance of the second outside hitter. They called it the *Crnich Factor.*

• Weston had eighteen kills, but her attack percentage of .040 was the lowest of her career. She did, however, lead the team with a personal record of twenty-two digs, showing leadership by not allowing her relatively low attack percentage affect her dominant performances in blocking and floor defense. One of those digs was spectacular and came with Texas's serving to win the fourth game at 14-13. It was a play she would not have made had we not made defense the focus of our season by having players dig a hundred balls at the beginning of each practice.

• Jen McFadden had one of the best matches of her career with a season high sixteen kills on a .414 hitting percentage and three blocks. It was the last match Jen would play for the Huskers as an off-season injury prevented her from playing what promised to be a spectacular senior season. Jen was an unusual talent who appeared to be more comfortable on the volleyball court than anywhere else in her life. She was a tremendous presence in the front row.

• Sophomore Lisa Reitsma had sixteen kills, five of them in the fourth game when the match was on the line. She became a three-time All-American and led the team back to the Final Four the next season despite the departure of four great players. She was the first player from a conservative Dutch Reformed community in southwest Iowa to take the risk of playing for a major university.

• Christy Johnson followed the game plan to perfection and played with such passion and enthusiasm that she received a couple of marriage proposals from volleyball fans watching the game on television. In her journal she writes of making a courageous 31 set to Jen McFadden as Texas was making a run in the fourth game. Her journal also reveals how devastated she would have been if the Huskers had lost and how it might have been a roadblock to her future. Her history of overcoming disappointments and challenges suggest otherwise. She is now the highly successful head volleyball coach at Iowa State University.

• The answer to a trivia question that all but the most ardent of Husker volleyball fans would miss is *Stacie Maser*. Stacie started each match of the season at the middle blocker position in the front row so that Jen McFadden could make her three entries later in the game. In 1995 there was no libero and a player could enter the game only three times. Maria Hedbeck, our strongest defensive player, would play in the back row for McFadden. Starting Stacie Maser allowed both Hedbeck and McFadden three entries. With the adoption of the libero and unlimited entries, a significant part of the tactical decisions of coaching volleyball has been removed.

• In the post-match press conference Texas coach Mick Haley closed with the following remark: *"This is a great experience for our team, but I wonder if our players know how hard it is for seniors to lead a team while still playing well. Nebraska understands that."*

The Next Day

I slept on the flights from Hartford to Chicago and Chicago to Lincoln on the following morning, something I rarely do. I can be a nervous flyer, but the championship matches and the preparation for them had left me exhausted. When we arrived at the Lincoln airport we were escorted to the Coliseum where 3,000 Husker volleyball fans were waiting to share in the celebration.

I do not remember much of what was said. I know that the three seniors and I each spoke for a few minutes and a small band played the Nebraska fight song. I remember carrying Emma, our youngest daughter who was 18 months old, onto to the stage with me and handing her to Katherine just before I spoke.

Later, the team adjourned to the locker room and hung out for a few minutes. There were no speeches or anything dramatic, just a group of people who were relaxing in the special feeling of having completed a remarkable journey. One by one people departed the locker room until only Kate Crnich and I were sitting in chairs next to each other.

It was then that I asked her, "Kate, what happened? How were you able to have one of the best matches in NCAA history?" She said two things that I will always remember. Kate replied: "It was when you came to me in practice and told me not to worry about all the technical things and that I was already good enough. That changed things for me." After a few seconds she continued, "I didn't want to let my teammates down."

Those two sentences are a pretty good summary of what I know about team-building. But here is another truth: While I might eventually have come to the decision on my own to reassure Kate and stop trying to fix her in practice, I might not have come to that insight until after the season had it not been for the conversation with David Cook. If John Cook had not shared the observation that Christy's sets were dying inside against Michigan State, I might not have made that adjustment in our practice preceding the championship match. If I had not envisioned the plaque in Frank Brown's kitchen that suggested I *ride the horse in the direction it was going,* I might not have had the patience to stick with setting our fourth and fifth options in a national championship match. I was mentored by collaborative leadership to some of the most important decisions that I made in a championship season.

Finale

I was awakened on my first morning at home following the tournament with a voice on the radio saying, *"No wind fills the sails of a ship without direction."* It's an anonymous quote that had direct application to the championship season. What it meant to me was that if you don't have a specific destination, no amount of energy or tactical skill is going to help you. But if you know where you are going, you don't have to take a straight line. You can tack and use every opportunity, every interaction, every practice, and every challenge as the energy to fill the sails of the ship.

A week later, the student newspaper interviewed Kate Crnich, perhaps the first time she was ever the focus of a newspaper article. Kate, the least analytical and least verbal of all of the players I ever coached, was quoted saying the most rewarding thing I've ever read about the culture created by Nebraska Volleyball. When asked by the reporter what kind of impact Nebraska Volleyball had on her college experience, she replied:

When I stepped on the Coliseum court for the first time, I sensed that something special was happening to me, and that I would never be the same again.

ABOUT THE AUTHOR

For twenty-three years Terry Pettit led one of the most successful NCAA athletic programs in history. During his tenure as head coach, the University of Nebraska women's volleyball team won twenty-one conference championships while leading the nation in All-American and Academic All-American selections. His teams were ranked in the Top 10 for the final sixteen years and advanced to the NCAA Championship Finals on six occasions, winning Nebraska's first national championship in volleyball in 1995. He received National Coach of the Year honors in 1986, 1994, and 1996.

Since 2005 Terry Pettit has been directing leadership academies at Creighton University, the University of Denver, and Colorado State University while mentoring coaches and athletic administrators throughout the country. He has also presented on leadership and team-building to many of the most successful and progressive corporations in the country. Graduating with a B.S. in English from Manchester College and an M.F.A. in poetry from the Creative Writing Workshop at the University of Arkansas, Terry Pettit has a unique perspective as a poet, educator, coach, and parent on team-building, leadership, and the challenges of coaching.

Terry lives in Fort Collins, Colorado, with his wife Anne, and their daughter, Emma.

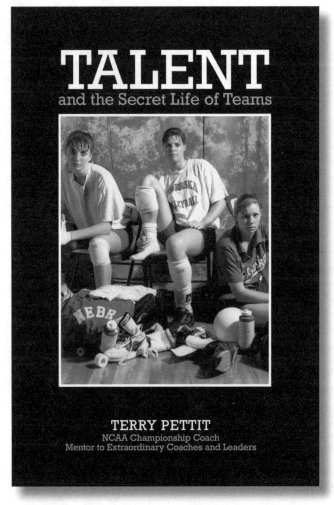

To order copies of this book, go online to:
www.terrypettit.com.

If you would like Terry Pettit to present
to your organization, please contact him at:
tpettit@terrypettit.com